Droppin Jewelz

GUIDING PRINCIPLES TO HELP GIRLS LIVE THEIR BEST LIFE

VOLUME 1: RUBY EDITION

Kendra Hall

Life On Purpose Publishing
SAN ANTONIO, TEXAS

Edited by: Dr. Angela D. Massey
Cover by: pixelstudios
Photography by: Manley Photography

For permission requests, contact the Author at the address below.

Kendra Hall
www.droppinjewelz.com
wearejewelz@gmail.com

Ordering Information:
Quantity sales. Special discounts are available on quantity purchases by corporations, associations, and others. For details, contact the "Special Sales Department" at the electronic address above.

Droppin' Jewelz/ Kendra Hall. —Vol. 1. Ruby Edition
ISBN: 978-0-692-18902-3
LCN: 2018959509

Contents

This book is dedicated to my best friend forever: the super talented, ambitious, wise and beautiful Andrea Ray. Your resilient spirit is always near. I will always honor your memory. I am my sister's keeper.

"Life is all about the journey. We will all have successes and failures; however, we must endure."

—KENDRA HALL

Droppin' Jewelz

GUIDING PRINCIPLES TO HELP GIRLS LIVE THEIR BEST LIFE

VOLUME ONE: RUBY EDITION

Kendra Hall

Introduction

Taking care of a child when you are still a child, is no easy task. It's even harder when you lack the proper support and mindset to handle the adult challenges of life. You may feel unprepared, scared, lonely and not know what to do to get your life back on track. In this book you will meet such a person, Corrine, who became a mother when she was 14. She was competing for spots in other people's lives, not realizing that hers was the only spot that mattered. Corinne's poor choices came with a heavy price to pay. She learned to trust in God the hard way.

Your course in life will require you to make decisions that may yield heavy consequences. We need to be able to identify what love looks like. The only way we can do that is if we know God's love as our model. It is imperative that you learn to know, trust and love yourself.

There is power in the Infinite Spirit. Sometimes you get lured off your course. But fear not, you will move from barely making it, to having more than enough. God will speak to the right people in your favor, and open supernatural doors for you. Just know that every next level will demand a different version of you. Life is all about the journey.

We will all have successes and failures; however, we must endure. Now, let's see what rubies we can pick up along Corrine's journey.

Kendra Hall

CHAPTER ONE

Enough

An older woman walks into a restaurant and goes to the closest table. She places her heavy bags on the white tiled floor and scoots into the snug chair. She has been running errands since early morning and has taken a break to get coffee and a Danish before continuing with her day.

The restaurant is almost deserted. A tired waitress walks over to the women to take her order. The waitress holds a piping hot pot of coffee in her right hand and begins to fill the woman's mug. The steaming hot coffee cup begins to fill almost automatically as its deep aroma tickles her nostrils. In a low voice, the waitress states, "Let me know when it's enough, Ma'am." The coffee twists around the brim of the cup. It starts to overflow and splatter onto the table making a mess. The woman, who was only half-paying attention in the first place, notices she let the waitress pour the coffee too long before telling her she'd had enough. She turns the corners of her mouth up, showing off a warm smile and tells the waitress she should have been more attentive. She should have told her, "Enough."

The waitress asked the woman to let her know when she had enough coffee in her cup. The problem was the older woman was exhausted. She was not giving her attention to the coffee and expected the waitress to pay attention and let her know when the cup was filled, not the other way around.

The woman was much like Corrine, my next-door neighbor who had her first child just a few days after her fourteenth birthday. Corrine was the mother of three when she turned eighteen. For a large portion of her life Corrine sat in silence, putting the responsibility on others to notice when her cup was full. Just like the overflowing cup of coffee, she was susceptible to what people poured into her—we all are. We hope they will see what they are doing and stop when it is too much. The reality of the situation is more than likely people will keep dumping more and more into your cup if you do not speak up for yourself.

Losing Control

When people do not speak up for themselves, they run into trouble because they lose control of situations. That's how it happened with Corrine. Just a few years earlier she was a 12-year-old who had no time for boys. Her days consisted of schoolwork, church, chores and outside activities. Corinne was the youth group leader at church and lead singer in the children's choir. On Saturdays, she took professional acting lessons and eventually auditioned for a role on a major television show. She had already landed short roles on several television shows and was also auditioning for a role in the *Wizard of Oz* at school. On Thursdays she stayed late at school with her dance troupe in preparation for her solo. From the outside looking in, Corinne was a model child who had it all together. But that was very far from the truth. Corinne was looking for excitement—the kind of excitement she read about in the *R.L. Stine* books she was obsessed with.

Walking through the halls of junior high that day she had no clue she would meet a person to whom she would allow to have such power over her life. She had no idea that she would become the person who didn't know how to say enough.

Kristen, Corrine's best friend, wanted her to meet Travis, Kristen's favorite cousin who transferred to their school from the South. It seemed every time Corinne and Kristen spoke, Travis's name had to be slipped into the conversation. Kristen talked about how Travis had all the girls, how tough Travis was, blah, blah, blah. Whenever Kristen spoke about Travis, Corinne would just roll her eyes. Corinne hadn't met Travis yet, but she wondered what all the hype was about. The way Kristen spoke you would think Travis was a superstar or teen idol. Corinne remained unimpressed and shrugged off any thought of Kristen's cousin—that is until she met him.

A rush of air seemed to move toward Corinne the day she looked up just in time to meet Travis's unwavering stare. Travis's piercing grey eyes sent a strange tingle up her spine. "Who is he?" Corinne asked herself. It was at that moment

Travis took steps to close the distance between them. He walked closer to Corinne and before she knew it, Travis had brushed her right cheek and was whispering in her ear for her to call him, all while stuffing a piece of paper in her pocket and walking off. Everything happened so fast. Corinne felt like the air had been knocked out of her. She looked at the piece of paper in her pocket and read, "Call me. Travis." She shook her head in disbelief. This had to be Kristen's Travis. Corinne thought of the words "Kristen's Travis" and realized at that very moment she would rather be saying "Corinne's Travis." She smiled inside.

At home, Corinne knew that she could not have Travis call her. Her parents (mainly her father) had decided that maybe boys could call when she was 16, which was four years away. At 12, there didn't seem to be many things Corinne could decide for herself. The one thing she felt she had control over was her growing feelings for Travis. Corinne dreamt about the two of them as if they were in a Disney fairytale. Travis was always her Prince Charming.

Corinne felt like she was her happiest when she was with Travis. He seemed to always improve any mood she was in and make her heart smile. He was always very kind and cheery. She loved their conversations about how he was going to marry her, and they were going to live in his aunt's huge house in the South. Travis was always planning their future and telling her she needed to start picking out her wedding dress because they were going to get married soon. Travis told Corinne they would run away and go somewhere it was legal for them to get married. After all, Corinne was only 12 and Travis was barely 13. They were not at an age where they could legally make any major decisions. However, a short year later, they inadvertently made the decision to have a baby.

"It wasn't intentional" Corinne thought, as she reflected on how she got pregnant. Hiding her relationship with Travis was challenging for Corinne. They had to come up with creative ways to see each other, like staying after school. Or meeting in the library. Corinne would have Travis come to her Youth Bible Study on Wednesdays because it always ended early, giving her and Travis free time in the parking lot for at least a half hour until Adult Bible Study ended. In fact, she and Travis shared their first kiss behind the church van in the parking lot.

Corinne felt a feeling she had never felt before. She felt alive and in control. Having control was the one thing she craved. It seemed as if Corinne's whole life was decided for her and she never had time to do the things she wanted to do. She felt trapped and being with Travis was the only thing that made her feel free and in control.

Travis was always so sweet to her. Plus, if anyone dared bother Corinne, Travis was like a pit bull. Kids feared yet respected Travis because he had the reputation of being a great fighter. Even though Travis was tough, he always made Corinne feel loved and protected. Eventually the topic of sex came up and while she was a 12-year-old child unfamiliar with her own body, his kisses made her feel like a woman. She reasoned that she had control over her body and so she decided to lose her virginity to Travis.

The thought of losing her virginity frightened the 12-year-old. Despite her fears, Corrine wanted to show Travis how important he was to her. She wanted him to know that she could not imagine her life without him and if having sex proved that, she was all in.

Pump the Brakes

As a young adult I owned a car that seemed to always need brakes. It seemed like every time I replaced my brakes, they were in need again. I would always be on edge while coming to streets with stop signs. My heart would race as I would hear the sharp scraping noise of the poorly functioning brakes. I would pray my car stopped in time, hold my breath, grip the side of the door, and hope I wouldn't cause an accident. I knew I needed brakes no matter the cost. I could not live with the fear of being hit and I wanted to have my peace of mind back. I was stressed out worrying about my poorly functioning brakes.

One thing I could not imagine was not having brakes at all. It didn't matter what my car looked like or how it sounded; all that mattered was I needed to get my brakes repaired as soon possible. There was no need for me to put myself or others at risk and possibly end my life by not having brakes. We all need brakes in life as they serve an important purpose.

You must apply control and influence over yourself. When you do not exhibit control over yourself and the situations that occur in your life, you give up your power and become an observer in your own life story. You wish things will get better in your life as opposed to acting to ensure your wishes come to fruition. You can hope and wish all you want, without control you can't control the brakes and navigate your life in the direction it is destined to go.

Like Corrine, there are times we may want to give other people the reigns to our lives. It can feel easier at times to just let another person make the hard decisions while you just sit back and enjoy the ride. God has already given you the compass for your life. It's disrespectful to you and God to allow another person to determine your life's route; that's God's responsibility. You are giving someone else too much power over you. This is the life God gave you. Honor it. Those other people must drive their own vehicle. They have their own journey. There is not an acceptable excuse you could give yourself to justify giving your power away. You will meet many people who will try their best to give you direction and they may, overall, mean well; but, remember the compass for *your* life belongs to you. Use it.

Regaining Control

So, how do you use your compass? Corrine, still an adolescent, set the compass of her life to destination: teenage motherhood. She lost control before she was given the proper guidance to know she even had control.

When I speak of control, I'm talking about taking responsibility for controlling your life, especially if you find yourself in a place where you have lost it. To regain control, you must accept this simple, yet profound truth: Only you can control yourself, no one else! You cannot make anyone feel a certain way or think a certain thing. The only person you can focus on is you. As Corrine's story unfolds, you will see that for most of her young life her focus was misplaced. In a futile attempt to be loved and accepted, she allowed Travis and others to control her—she became a classic people-pleaser.

People Pleasing

Many times, we do things that do not speak to our sense of purpose but more to please another person. The emphasis is placed on putting a smile on another person's face and making them happy, no matter the cost. We put so much stock into what someone else thinks, until we can't make a move unless we consult with person first. We are too busy making sure we are pleasing the other person and that they are happy, but what about our happiness? Having a helping spirit within you is beautiful; however, if you are always looking for a pat on the back from others as opposed to putting energy into your path, you will fail at life.

Who's the Real God in Your Life?

My main point is the only thoughts you need to take into consideration are those of the Infinite Spirit. Your job is to be pleasing to God, not man. He is the one that needs to be given preferential treatment; he gets all the glory and honor. There is no one above Him and it is time you fully recognize that. When you spend your time trying to be a people pleaser and put too much emphasis on what others think, you make them the gods of your life. You have inadvertently ordained these people to represent the false gods of your life.

Don't be concerned about what others think about you, it's none of your business anyway. Who cares? To maintain control over your life you must keep in the forefront of your mind that God has given you a special purpose. After all, you are beautifully and wonderfully made. You have the plan that God has given you and nothing else matters. Nothing.

Sometimes we lack control over our lives because we are scared and lack confidence. We ask ourselves, "Who would listen to me anyway?" Our lack of confidence paralyzes us with fear. It's at these times we must take a deep breath and remember our rightful place in this world. "God has not given us the spirit of fear but of power and love and of a sound mind." (NKJV) You are meant to be seen and heard. It is your birthright to have a magnanimous life.

Take a stand and speak up for yourself. There is no fear in standing in your truth. Don't worry about people leaving you if you stop trying to please them. You cannot please everyone, but you certainly need to please yourself first. If a person wants to leave . . . let them leave! These are the same people who have been using and abusing you. There is no reason for them to stay around you any longer. They may be mad they no longer have control over you. You may have allowed people to have power over you so long that they now feel like they own you. You fed their ego when you gave them your power, when you wouldn't or couldn't say, "Enough!" Now they will do or say anything to you to maintain that powerful feeling.

There are people who will disregard you, even when you say you have had enough. They will not care that you say you have had enough and they will not respect any boundary you set. Some people will come into your life to test you to see if you love them more then you love yourself. They are disrespectful and not worth the drama, conversation or confrontation. Say nothing and leave the person where they are. You can only control yourself and you do not need the extra drama or stress in your life. You have no time to waste on dead situations. Remember, God will neither leave you nor forsake you. Focus on controlling yourself and following the plan He has for you and learn how to let people know when you've had enough.

CHAPTER GEMS

- Never rely on another person to drive you through life.
- You can only control yourself, no one else!
- People will keep dumping more and more into your cup if you do not speak up for yourself.
- For you to be your best self and complete the journey God has placed before you, it's imperative you take total control over your life.
- Take a stand and speak up for yourself. There is no fear in standing in your truth.
- Take full control of yourself so you can ascend to greatness.
- Your job is to be pleasing to God, not man.
- Use your God-given compass to decide the direction of your life.
- Focus on controlling yourself and following the plan God has for you.
- Learn how to let people know when you've had enough.

YOUR GEMS

(How can you use the lessons in this chapter in your life? Use this page to write down your ideas, and insights.)

CHAPTER TWO

Decisions and Consequences

When John Stossel, co-author of an article entitled *Sex in Middle School?*[1] asked 13-year-old Anya Alvarez why girls feel pressured to become sexually active at such young ages, she replied, "because guys don't need girls' approval, but girls need guys' approval." I believe it goes even deeper than Anya's astute observation. The Bible says it is not good for man to be alone. Our need for companionship goes back to when God created Eve from Adam's rib. God saw Adam was lonely and created Eve to be his companion. He instructed Adam and Eve to be fruitful and multiply. Clearly, God never meant for us to isolate ourselves from others. However,

[1] https://abcnews.go.com/2020/story?id=123789&page=1

when a young girl looks for companionship before she matures and understands her value, like Corrine she is bound to seek the wrong kind of companionship with the wrong company at the wrong time. Corrine's parents failed to communicate to Corrine her value; so, she chose to seek validation from Travis—a choice that would have grave consequences.

Sex educator Deborah Roffman, author of Sex and Sensibility: The Thinking Parent's Guide to Talking Sense About Sex advises, ". . . sexual intercourse is the most fundamentally powerful behavior there is on the face of the Earth. It's a behavior that has the ability to do the three most powerful things there are, all at the same time. It has the ability to give life, potentially take life away and to change it forever. That's unbelievably powerful and therefore, it shouldn't be in the hands of anybody who isn't an adult, in as many ways as they need to be an adult. It's not for kids."

Family Fallout: 13 and Pregnant

A few months after losing her virginity, Corinne realized she may be pregnant. She missed her period and was trying to figure out what to do. Corinne told Travis and he had his older sister pick up a pregnancy test and bring it to the school. He waited outside the girl's bathroom for the results. Finally, Corinne slowly walked out of the bathroom and looked Travis in the eyes. Travis knew by the look on Corinne's face he was going to be a father. "I'm going to be a father!" His excitement at the news somehow eased her fears—at least momentarily. At that moment, nothing and no one mattered to her except Travis and their baby.

It was getting harder for Corinne to hide her growing belly from her family. Rumors were swirling around school and she knew it was only a matter of time before the adults in her life found out. In fact, some adults already knew like Ms. Stephenson, her school counselor who gave her an ultimatum: Corinne had to tell her parents or Ms. Stephenson was going to tell them. It was the day it rained almost as if God himself was crying about the predicament she had gotten herself into. Anxiety gripped Corrine as she wondered what her parents would do to her. She was scared to tell them and not even the thought of Travis eased her mind.

The rain stopped briefly, but the sun refused to shine. There seemed to be a grey overcast covering the sky as Corinne walked home after Ms. Stephenson's ultimatum: "Tell your parents today. If you don't, I will tell them tomorrow!" She entered the foyer and was greeted by her mother, Dianne, who was home from work early that day. Corrine didn't even have time to collect her thoughts.

Corinne told her mother that she had something to talk to her about. Dianne asked what it was; in reply, Corinne simply asked her to sit down. Dianne smiled at her daughter trying to be a grown up. Dianne had barely sat down before Corrine blurted out, "I'm pregnant." Dianne stood up slowly, trying to process the words coming out of her 13-year-old daughter's mouth. There was no way in hell her child just told her that she was pregnant! How and when? Dianne thought. Between church and extracurricular activities, she could not imagine when Corinne's pregnancy could have occurred. Maybe her daughter had been molested, but by whom?

"Did someone hurt you?"

"No," Corrine replied, hoping her matter-of-fact tone would let her mother know that she knew exactly what she was doing.

"How did this happen? Who's the father?"

"I have a boyfriend and we skipped school."

"How many times did you skip school to have sex?" Dianne spat the word "sex" out as though she had bitten into Aunt Mabel's fruitcake by mistake. Dianne didn't like Aunt Mabel, and she hated fruitcake.

"It only happened once. It was the first time I had sex." Corrine's voice trailed off, barely audible when she said the word "sex." In that moment all her bravado vanished and saying it made her feel dirty and ashamed. She continued, "It was the first time and I got pregnant."

What luck, Dianne thought. "Who is the father?" Dianne demanded, her voice shrill and high pitched.

"I have a picture of him," Corinne said and proceeded to pull out last year's school yearbook.

Dianne looked at Travis's picture in disbelief. She could not believe this young knuckle head had gotten her 13-year old daughter pregnant. She slammed the yearbook closed and told Corinne that her relationship with Travis was over, and that she was taking her to get an abortion. Corinne clutched her stomach at the thought of her losing her baby. She told herself that she would not lose her child.

Dianne placed the responsibility of telling Harold, her husband and Corinne's father, about the pregnancy on Corrine. Harold was very controlling; he didn't take well to unpleasant news, and he and Corinne had never enjoyed a great relationship. Both Dianne and Corrine knew that this news would send him over the top.

When Harold walked into the house he was greeted by the tear-stained faces of his wife and daughter.

"What's wrong?"

"Have a seat, Harold," Dianne's wide-sweeping motion indicated that he was free to sit wherever he wanted.

"I'll stand. What is it?" Harold demanded as he puffed out his chest out. Dianne looked at Corinne for a response.

"I'm pregnant," Corinne confessed.

"The hell you are pregnant!" roared Harold, and at that moment, he forcefully rushed towards her only to be intercepted by Dianne. "Harold, no!" Dianne screamed out. "You need to calm down."

He could not believe his ears. His 13-year-old daughter was pregnant. Maybe she was attacked. "Were you raped?" Harold asked Corinne. "No, I was not raped, Corinne stated in a monotone that seemed to whisper, "I wish I was dead." He threw his hands up in the air in frustration.

"How could you do this to me, to this family? I've supplied you with all the opportunities in the world and this is what you do with your life . . . just throw it away?" It was clear to Corrine that he wasn't expecting any answers, so she just sat there while her father ranted. Harold thought of how he could get his daughter out of this situation and lessen the impact of embarrassment it would have on the family.

"We're taking you to the doctor first thing in the morning to see what the options are. And do know, there is no way you will have a baby in my house! You are only to use disposable plates, cups and utensils until we get a clean bill of health from the doctor because your fast behind self probably got AIDS! And stay in your room because I can't stand the sight you!"

Corrine obeyed.

Options

Doctor Frederickson told Corinne and her parents that abortion was not an option as the pregnancy was too far along. She sighed, relieved and happy at the thought of keeping her baby, but careful not to let it show. Meanwhile, Harold and Dianne were seething. The whole situation had spun their lives completely around and her father tried his best to think of a solution that would put his household back in the order he demanded of himself, his wife, and his children.

Harold showed Corinne a video clip of a place in Oklahoma for pregnant girls. He told her that she would stay at this school until she gave birth and then immediately put the child up for adoption.

"Go to Oklahoma. Put that 'bastard' you're carrying up for adoption. God will forgive your sins. But if you decide to keep it, you will no longer be a part of this family, so you better think long and hard about this. And since you think you're grown, I expect an answer first thing tomorrow."

Corinne really needed no time to make her decision. She took one look at the miserable-looking girls wearing long old-fashioned skirts and knew without a doubt she didn't want to go to that school.

The next day Harold burst into Corinne's room demanding her decision. Corinne quietly told him she neither wanted to go away to the girls' school nor did she want to give her baby up for adoption. I mean, how could she give her baby up? She was finally going to have someone to love her unconditionally. While she was scared, she was also oddly happy. Harold was furious.

"Get out of this house! You will be living poor from now on and the kids in ghetto are going to beat your behind. You're a whore and I hate you," Harold fumed with rage, "I should spit in your face!"

TOXIC RELATIONSHIPS

Writers at teenpregnancystatistics.org advise, "It can be difficult to get over the strong feelings that can accompany a teen pregnancy. [Parents] may want to lash out. However, it is quite likely that the teenager is already painfully aware of her mistake and wishes to move on with life. Shunning her may only lead to more heartbreak down the road. It's up to you [parents] whether you will help her overcome this mistake and make something of her life, or whether you will abandon her."[2]

[2] http://www.teenpregnancystatistics.org/content/parental-support-of-pregnant-teens.html

Perhaps you are facing abandonment and the one place you looked to for support no longer exists. You must be able to identify which relationships work for you and which do not. There are ways to recognize relationships that do not serve our highest good. Toxic relationships that are easy to spot are ones that have constant issues and are always filled with drama. The two of you disagree constantly. You argue with the person all the time and half of the time you don't know what you are even arguing about. You feel like the other person is always at opposition with you and always wants to fight. In Corrine's case, it seemed that she and her father never got along. When she was a baby, she cried too much. When she was six, she was too opinionated. He was always right, and he shut down anyone who dared to disagree.

These types of toxic relationships drain your energy, leaving you feeling lifeless. You invest so much time and energy into the other person, until you have no energy left for yourself. It's not worth it. Ask yourself how much further you would be in life if you were not wasting time arguing and being on the defensive. Toxic relationships destroy your hopes and dreams and promote an overall sense of failure. They make you feel miserable and prevent you from living up to your true potential. These relationships act as the arch nemeses to your greatness. When you discover you are too preoccupied with defending your position and are constantly in baseless arguments, it's time to cut your losses. The question is how can you do this when you are faced with becoming a parent before you become an adult?

Before I drop some jewelz of wisdom on this topic, remember that there are some super stressful relationships in your life, but you must fight to maintain them. The relationship between parent and child is one of those relationships. In the book of Ephesians 6:1-4. God commands that we honor our mother and father. In the same vein, the Bible states parents are to love their children unconditionally and greet them with open arms. Parents are to lead by example; yet, sometimes this does not happen. Maybe you have a dad like Harold. He refuses to acknowledge you or your baby and takes your pregnancy as a personal attack on him and all that he stands for. Maybe you have a mom like Dianne . . . silently suffering as her domineering husband treats you poorly. I know what I'm about to tell you will be hard to understand: despite the hell your parents may put you through, don't harden your heart towards them.

And if you're not already, one day you may get married, so understand that you may go through a rough patch. It's natural to have ups and downs in marriage. Remember, you have made a covenant with God that you will work through the good and bad times with your spouse. Make sure you speak to your spouse with an open heart. Try to understand your spouse's viewpoint. Look for a spiritual mentor if you must. The exception to any of this advice is if you are being abused. If you are being beaten and abused, you need to leave.

How to Get Out of Toxic Relationships

Look for relationships that act as a conduit to peace and love. To move forward, you must place yourself around people who want to see you win. Relationships do not have to be explosive, filled with drama, and drag you down. You must let go of relationships that do not promote your success. There is no need to fight and argue with anyone all the time. Don't deal with drama when you do not have to.

You can enjoy a person because you feel comfortable around them. You may share childhood memories, laugh together, and reminisce on days long past. The person is likened to your favorite pair of old slippers. The slippers have lost their cushioning and don't offer much beyond a sense of familiarity. The slippers are not getting better and as time passes, you notice they are getting less comfortable. You love your slippers and cannot imagine giving them up. After all, the slippers have been a part of your life a long time. The problem is these slippers will not hold up on your next journey. The soles are already coming apart. Just as your old familiar relationship is comfortable, so are your worn slippers. You must decide to let go of what is familiar to embrace the unfamiliar. If all you share are memories, then how can you progress? Your need for comfort is keeping you in a dead place. You have moved into a new place and it's time to let go off the roots of your past. You deserve to be in a place of growth. You also deserve a pair of new slippers.

Another lesson I want to pass on is this: just because a person feels good *to* you, it does not mean they are good *for* you. You can reminisce on the good ole' days, rooted in who you used to be. I would rather connect with someone who shares my current goals. Sharing common goals leads to a shared purpose. Shared goals encourage you to work together as a team to achieve a result. It is comforting to share memories of playing hop scotch and tag as children; however, what is this person doing right now? Do you share any common goals with this person? If not, why are they still around? Ask yourself if you are making the most of your life if you can't grow with a person you are giving your energy to. It is a difficult realization to acknowledge a once revered relationship has transformed into dead weight.

You are in a unique position. You are either a teenaged parent or you're soon to be a teenaged parent. People from your past often have a preconceived notion of who you are based on old viewpoints you may no longer share. They see you as a cheerleader, a member of the Glee Club, or one of the friends who gather at the local pizza joint on the weekend. You aren't that person anymore; however, they are looking at you through clouded lens and cannot see you. Familiarity breeds contempt. These people saw you grow up and although you have grown, they cannot get those old images out of their mind. They have chosen to be unreceptive to your personal growth. Some people will refuse to accept anything about you except what they believe they "knew."

Don't be held down with those that "knew" you. You will be stuck, frozen in time and held back from your greatness. You are living in the present; the past is no more. People who cannot see your growth or your potential, must be removed from your life. I know it's a difficult thing to do, but your path to greatness needs to stay clear of baggage. You are a parent now and while you may still be a teenager, you can still be a successful person. You must be courageous and know when to drop the dead weight so that something better can take its place. You cannot allow another person to have you stuck in your past. No more talking about your days of playing hop scotch, it's time for you to get focused on the present. No more energy should be put into rehashing the old, you have new stories to be create.

Wolves in Sheep's' Clothing

The most harmful relationship is the one you cannot detect. There are people in the world that actively look to steal others joy. They are wolves in sheep's clothing. You will not recognize them as wolves until it's too late. These individuals are seemingly sweet, charismatic and kind. They bombard us with false love in the forms of gifts, flattery, and heartfelt promises. They make us feel alive and cause our heart to skip a beat.

I am sure you know people who act like this. They tell you all the things you want to hear and do the things you like to gain your trust. Another glimpse into Corrine's life will show you what I mean.

The day after Corrine told her father she didn't want to give her baby up for adoption, he sent her to live with Lorraine, her grandmother. Lorraine had agreed to allow Corrine to live with her, and enroll her in a transitional school for pregnant teens and high school dropouts. Once the baby was born, her grandmother would watch the child to allow Corinne to finish school.

Corinne started her new school as the only 8th grader until Lauren came. Lauren was a slender 14-year old with a very pregnant belly who wore the nicest clothes, accented by a great hairstyle and manicured nails. Corinne had never seen a girl like Lauren before. Every word that came out of Lauren's mouth seemed to exude confidence and they instantly became friends.

Around that time, Corinne started to get attention from Kyle, the senior class president. He started with compliments telling her that he loved the way she pronounced each word and that he could stare into her eyes all day. Corinne couldn't lie, she loved Kyle's attention and his flattering conversation. He wanted to know if she was still with her baby's father and since she answered yes, he asked if the two of them could at least be friends. He even told Corinne that he wanted to help her once her baby was born.

Lauren didn't like Kyle and advised Corinne that Kyle was a pervert and she should stay away from him.

Corinne giggled and asked, "Why do feel like that? Why don't you like him? He's nice."

"Kyle is too damn old to be hanging around you!" Lauren was sounding more like Corrine's mother, stern and matter-of-fact. The "damn" only made her sound more grown up.

"He's only 17," Corrine said innocently. True enough she was about to become a mother, however, most of the time her lack of maturity dominated her thought process and spilled over into her conversations.

Lauren stared at Corinne with a look of bewilderment, "As matter of fact that 'old man' is nothing short of 23 years old. He has no business being around you at all. Girl, plus he is broke, so please stay away from him, he probably got worms! Furthermore, I don't like the way Dude looks at you, it gives me the creeps. Just be careful around him."

Corinne thought Lauren was overreacting, especially after she threatened to tell the teacher if she saw Kyle talking to Corrine again. Corinne couldn't believe Lauren was acting this way. She thought Lauren had her back and now she was threatening to tell the teacher on her for no reason. Corinne did not like that at all.

One day Kyle insisted that they take a walk to the store for lunch. He said Corinne had been such a good friend to him and he wanted to treat her. Lauren wasn't in school that day, so Corinne agreed. Plus, Corinne was hungry!

As Kyle and Corinne walked to the store to get lunch, it seemed like they were passing stores instead of going into one. Corinne asked him how far the store was because it was hot outside, her ankles were swollen, and she was starving. He said that he had forgotten something at his brother's house. Corinne wanted to go back to school, but he insisted since they were just seconds away from his brother's apartment and he would make her something to eat.

As Corinne walked through the projects, it seemed like everyone was outside. Kyle asked that if he could hold Corinne's hand because there were rocks on the ground and he didn't want her to fall. Corinne innocently complied.

Upon entering a tiny studio apartment, Kyle's offered Corinne a glass of juice. The offer was right on time because Corinne felt like she was dying of thirst. Once Corinne took a sip of her juice, she felt Kyle's hands firmly grip her around her waist, throwing her on the bed. It was then that Corinne realized she should have heeded Lauren's warning. Corinne had to fight Kyle off to keep him from raping her. Thankfully, she nor her unborn child were harmed.

Kyle was the wolf dressed as a sheep, but Corrine was blind to who he truly was. He manipulated her with false words and acceptance. He wanted to win her trust, because as wolf he only saw her as prey.

Wolves are like the school classmates that say nice things about you to your face but speak unkindly behind your back. They want to make themselves look good and will use your back as a stepping stone. You will find boyfriends who promise you the world, with no intention to love you. There will be fake friends who are hiding their true animosity towards you. You could be talking to your fake friend about your boyfriend's infidelity, and the fake friend may be the one secretly cheating with your man. Be vigilant. Don't put things past people. Some people are not your friends, they are just scared to openly be your enemy. You don't know what demons they are struggling with. It's no secret most people act in their own self-interest. However, the wolves of the world take things to another level. These individuals feel clever when they deceive people. They have closed themselves off to God.

It's imperative you know and accept that some people come into your life to cause you harm. Their tongues spew poison that drips out their mouth like honey. They know the right words to unlock your heart. They offer fake love, baseless power, money, and whatever they can say to gain entrance into your world. We feast on their lies because they make us feel special and valued. We enjoy the position we have in their lives and begin to tie their fake love to our sense of self-worth. Somehow, we forget that God had already established our value. He is the alpha and omega in our world. Be aware of charismatic people because the version of them you crafted in your head may not exist. Always remember this: You are God's child and you do not need men to exalt you.

CHAPTER GEMS

- You must be able to identify which relationships work for you and which don't.
- You have real friends and fake friends. Separate yourself from the fake ones.
- Toxic relationships drain your energy, leaving you feeling hopeless.
- Despite the hell your parents may put you through, don't harden your heart towards them.
- Look for a spiritual mentor.
- Place yourself around people who want to see you win.
- Don't deal with drama when you do not have to.
- You must decide to let go of what is familiar to embrace the familiar.
- Just because a person feels good to you, it does not mean they are good for you.
- People who cannot see your growth or your potential must be removed from your life.

YOUR GEMS

(How can you use the lessons in this chapter in your life? Use this page to write down your ideas, and insights.)

CHAPTER THREE

Fixed Windows

A fixed window is a window that cannot be opened. It is ornamental . . . only for show with little or no functionality. It seemed that for most of her young life Corrine was surrounded by fixed windows.

A few days after her fourteenth birthday while preparing to sleep in Lorraine's hot, rat-infested basement, Corinne's water broke. She was eight months pregnant and Lorraine dropped her off at the emergency room never to return. It was the day Sean was born when she realized she was completely alone. Not just alone in the hospital, but alone in life. She had no plan and no clue as to what to do next. Her life was a fixed window—she could see out, but she wasn't able to get out.

Corrine, now a mom, was too young to realize that you must be purposeful in your journey. I recall going Easter egg hunting at the park with my friends as a child. We were given a map with clues and told we had to find a certain number of eggs to win a prize. My friends and I decided to work together to find the Easter eggs and divide the prize amongst us. We split up and looked in our assigned section of the park. Once we found the egg we were assigned to find, we would help the next friend find their egg. We had so much fun racing across the freshly cut grass. The tallest among us reached high into the tops of shrubbery looking for clues while the smallest investigated small crevices hoping to find any white oblong object.

Take inventory of the people around you. Are they diverse and focused on a common goal? Are you traveling with people who prioritize your well-being? Do you feel valued and respected by these people? Do these people see the growth in you or do they hold you to past ways or old habits? Use your energy to focus on the relationships that grow and weed out the ones that do not. Once you have the right team in your corner, you will soon experience greater joy in your everyday experiences. However, if you fail to have the support you need, your life will spiral out of control just as Corrine's did.

The Spiral

The doctors and nurses told Corrine that Sean was underweight with a touch of jaundice; but, he was overall in good condition. He weighed all of four pounds. He was her tiny and perfect miracle especially since pregnant women aged 14-17 years are at higher risk of preterm birth and of having a child with low birth weight[3]. The doctor explained that Corinne would be released from the hospital in a few days; but her son would need to stay in the hospital for another week or two, so she used the hospital phone to call Travis. He and his sister, Candance, stole their grandmother's car and drove to the hospital to see Corrine and Sean.

This was their new normal, two scrawny teenagers with an infant son. Travis told Corinne she would be able to live with him soon. He kissed her and left, calling her later to subdue her fears. With her discharge looming, Corinne had to deal with the fact that no one from her family had come to see or check on her. She did not know what to do. However, on her discharge day, her mother showed up looking weary and sad, there to explain that Corinne was no longer allowed to stay at Lorraine's. She did not want her there any longer. Lorraine was another fixed window. As an alternative, Dianne told Corinne that she and baby Sean would go live with her Aunt Belle, back in the suburbs.

She was happy and relieved to move in with Belle because she always treated Corinne as an equal. Aunt Belle used to live with her and her parents until Belle became pregnant as a teen and Harold kicked her out. Now 22, Belle had managed to make a home for herself and her child.

Corinne briefly found peace at Belle's house. The two of them would stay up late talking about their family, their men, and their babies. Belle even agreed to allow Travis to visit with Corrine and baby Sean. Corinne felt grown up now and

---

[3] www.sciencedaily.com/releases/2010/07/100708193446.htm

her body had filled out a bit in the right places. She was finally coming into her own.

Aunt Belle introduced Corinne to her crew of four girlfriends, two of whom were still seniors in high school. Lisa, Olivia, Jenna and Kara made up Belle's multicultural crew of girlfriends and quickly became Corinne's pretty girl crew.

Before long, Corrine was being dressed in tightly fitted clothing and high heels, caked in make-up and given a fake ID. Although she was only 14, she passed for 18 and went to some of New York's hottest night spots where she was introduced to men in their 20s and 30s. These men bought her gifts, took her out and showed her a lifestyle filled with fast cars and fast money. Corinne was their "diamond in the rough" that just needed their polishing.

Confrontations

Confrontations draw out a person's true essence. Confrontations allow us to see who people clearly are. We see what people are committed to. When we find a person is not committed to our highest good, we need to address that person through confrontation and reveal their true intentions. The scripture, 2 Timothy 1:7 (NIV) states, "the Spirit God gave us does not make us timid, but gives us power, love and self-discipline." We are not meant to be timid while confronting others. God's word has given us power and dominion.

Corrine faced such a confrontation and her perfect new world soon began to unravel. Belle was dealing with her son's abusive father who had started abusing her on a regular basis. She seemed to have horrible luck with men, but that should come as no surprise because she, as Corrine, had come into relationships with no one to guide and teach them what real love looked like. Not knowing what love looks like leaves you accepting the scraps of what love could be. Matters went from bad to worse when Corinne's mother showed up unexpectedly late one night and discovered Belle babysitting Sean, with Corinne nowhere to be found. It was then Corinne was whisked away to another journey.

Dianne informed Corinne she was to go into a shelter and that Sean would be placed up for adoption. Corinne told her mother that she would never allow her baby to be put up for adoption. She called Travis who, along with his father, came to pick her and Sean up from Belle's. It was then Corinne was reluctantly welcomed into Travis's family and, unbeknown to her, heightened levels of confusion and confrontation.

Confronting the Truth

During a confrontation, you may be faced with a hard truth about yourself. The hard truth for Corrine (and every other teenage mother for that matter) was that at 13 she was not prepared to be sexually active and at 14 she was not prepared to be a mother. We must be vulnerable and open to recognizing the truth. We are called to be reconciled to God and to each other, and we must do that through the Infinite Spirit.

Oftentimes parents of teenage mothers fail to see beyond the crisis, leaving the young mother without support, love, and encouragement. We may be looking at a person through pre-conceived notions and judgement. We blind ourselves to the potential for greatness lying dormant within the relationship. We need to look beyond our fears and be willing to see the gems within others. In an article entitled *A Teen Pregnancy in the Family*[4] the author suggests ways family members can see beyond their fears and see the gem within the situation:

Step into her shoes

- *Understand her fears. She is probably overwhelmed:*
- *Feeling like she has lost your love and confidence.*
- *Feeling alone and needing a support group.*
- *Wondering what her options are.*
- *Facing a future she hadn't planned.*

Step up

- *Be an asset to your daughter by:*
- *Reassuring her of your unconditional love and concern.*
- *Affirming your confidence in her.*
- *Trusting God whole-heartedly.*

Create a non-threatening atmosphere by:

- *Being willing to listen as she talks about her feelings.*
- *Giving advice only when asked.*
- *Enabling her to make rational, thoughtful decisions.*
- *Respecting her privacy. (Allow her to ponder secret thoughts.)*
- *Respecting her feelings about the baby's father (whether the relationship continues or is terminated).*
- *Guiding the baby's father into responsible participation.*

---

4 https://www.focusonthefamily.com/parenting/teens/your-teenager-is-pregnant/teen-pregnancy-in-family

Confrontations aim to clear problems or emotional and mental clutter. However helpful, we may not want to deal with confronting someone. We may put band-aids on matters instead of facing them with courage. If only Harold and Dianne had realized that by doing this, they were working backwards. They did not realize that their old ways would not give the new results. They had dealt with a teenage pregnancy with Belle and chosen to put her out. They repeated the same behavior with Corrine. Keep in mind that the amount of time and effort you put in will impact your result. It's time to try something new. Begin to see the relationship for what it is and could be.

Confrontation is not always about correcting someone who you feel is against you or assisting someone who you feel needs direction. It may be that you must agree to disagree or come to a compromise. You don't have to give up what you want for what the other person wants. There is no need to have to change who you are or change your beliefs. You can still walk in your truth. The prospect of compromise should not leave you feeling hopeless or defeated because you are scared, lazy or not in the mood.

The Art of Compromise

When you compromise with someone, and it's healthy, you realize the goal isn't about winning. You must be open, willing and put yourself in the other person's shoes. You must try to see things from their perspective. As a young girl, I remember loving to roller skate. I carried my shiny hot pink skates everywhere. I loved to put them on while at the grocery store shopping with my parents. One day I was roller-skating in the supermarket and accidently ran into the heels of another shopper. I felt awful that I had hurt someone. When I got home from the store, my parents told me I could skate everywhere except the grocery store. At the time, I didn't understand why I could not skate at the grocery store anymore just because I made one mistake. I could not, nor did I want to see their point of view. Although my parents didn't punish me by taking my skates or by telling me I couldn't skate at all, I still thought they were being excessive.

As an adult, an experience helped me finally see my parents' view point. I was shopping, minding my own business in the grocery store and while leaning forward to pick up a large box of cereal, a sharp pain hit the back of my right heel. "Sorry," a small voice hastily yelled out. A little boy was roller skating in the store. My first thought was a chastisement of the child's parents for allowing him to roller skate in the store. Soon after, I remembered being the child on the skates. God truly has a sense of humor! I learned it really hurts to have your heel run over by a roller skate. No one wants or deserves that! The child deserves to roller skate, but not when he is hurting someone or another's quality of life. A healthy compromise must be made.

There are times when you and the person both feel like you're right. You both know and trust that the other is coming from a loving spirit. You both may feel like you are speaking from a Godly based viewpoint or position. When you have this type of conflict, it can become confusing and frustrating. You both may want to say the other is wrong and leave it at that. However, this is the time to be humble. This is your test. Put your pride aside and step into the other persons shoes. Imagine your roles have reversed and take a brisk walk in their shoes. See if you can empathize with where they are coming from. Do you see their point yet? Can you understand why they feel the way they do? Is it possible for you to help them see your position using the same exercise?

You want a healthy compromise, so you can achieve a healthy relationship—that is the goal. God's grace and peace result from you gaining a clearer understanding of His word. There are times we are so focused on how we feel that we can't change. We can see the perfect example in how Harold and Dianne treated Corrine. We become stubborn and immovable. We act like we have all the answers, and no one can tell us anything new. This way of acting leads to stagnation. At the same time, we must know when not to compromise. Corrine felt strongly about not putting her baby up for adoption . . . there could be no compromise. We cannot allow people to impose their will upon us. We must be strong in our convictions and stay focused on God's word. We must stay focused on the things that matter; and by example, show others to do same.

When we become fluid to the ebbs and flows of life, we open ourselves up to kindness, openness and to finding progressive solutions. When we give our attention to the word of God, we are focusing on the things that matter the most. This focus helps us identify the things that do not matter easier. We must come to terms in our minds that some things just do not matter and do not warrant our attention. Always keep in that mind, compromise can be a good thing for both parties.

Recognizing Fixed Windows

There are some relationships that will thrive on open communication. You will see the relationship grow through the process of confrontation, open discussion and compromise. You feel warm and happy when you think of this relationship. Simultaneously, you are going to experience some relationships that will not improve no matter how hard you try. It will seem like something is off all the time and you will feel miserable. These relationships are, in effect, fixed windows.

When you discover a fixed window, take a minute to ponder why. Do you two share common goals? If not, the relationship may never work. You don't need to attend the same church, have the same social circle, go to the same school, have the same job or read the same books. However, you must have the same life ambitions and goals, or the relationship will be hard to maintain.

You need to be with people who understand you. You cannot walk with a person who competes with and does not cooperate with you. When someone competes with you, they are walking against you. When someone is walking in cooperation with you, they want to walk with you because by walking with you, they reach their goals faster.

Balanced Relationships

It's important to join with people who share our same passion and want to the same objective. I likened it to making a peanut butter and jelly sandwich. Without enough jelly, the consistency of the peanut butter will make the sandwich taste too thick. If you add too much jelly to the sandwich, it will taste too sweet. Both peanut butter and jelly are essential in creating a balanced taste. We need to create balanced relationships in our lives.

When we are in a relationship with a person who does not match our intensity, it can be frustrating. Imagine if you are working on a project with someone and are hyper focused on the task at hand. You notice your partner does not share your focus and is making careless mistakes. Your partner is not really interested in the task, and not giving it their full attention or effort. Now you must stop what you're doing to fix the other person's careless mistakes and you realize the whole situation has redirected your focus, making you less effective. You feel like you are dragging the other person along as they are less enthused and not committed to the project. You two are not in alignment and you become tired of trying to walk in harmony with them. You are spending time trying to motivate your partner to perform a task they have no real interest in; therefore, your partner will not invest significant effort. Your partner has made it clear by their actions that they really don't want to do the task in the first place. Now you have become exhausted from the entire interaction and feel like you lost the energy to complete the task. By having to continually refocus your partner, you are being counterproductive and not making efficient use of your time, energy or resources.

The Importance of Listening

It's important that you begin to listen to people. When you listen, you will be able to see who people really are. Most people will tell you who they are before you get involved, if you are willing to listen.

A friend of mine complained that she had gained 10 pounds over the summer and felt discouraged. She said she was always tired and felt unmotivated. I encouraged her to go to the gym. She said she wanted a gym partner to work out with her to help get her on the right track. That's when I told her I would go with her to the gym the next day. The next day I got dressed and prepared to meet her at the gym until I received a text from her saying she was too tired to go to the gym that morning. I replied by text okay, we could try the next day and she agreed. The next day my friend gave me another excuse as to why she could not work out. I became frustrated with the whole situation. However, as I reflected on our initial conversion, I realized she had previously warned me of her weaknesses. She had already told me she was tired and not feeling motivated. It's no wonder she did not want to go to the gym. So why was I frustrated? It made no sense for me to be annoyed. I should have put on my listening ears and paid attention to what my friend was saying.

It will save you pain, heartache, tears, frustration, agony, and disappointment when you master the art of listening. People know themselves best, so listen to what they have to say about themselves.

When we don't listen to people, we will find ourselves in energy draining relationships that can last a lifetime. It's important to remember that anyone you must motivate to get started will also have to be motivated to keep going. This is true for all the relationships in your life. These types of relationships demand a lot of your energy. You need to surround yourself with those that share your motivations, goals, and desires.

Find an Open Window

When you are around people who do not care about your goal, it can be deadly. If a person is not interested or does not care about your goal, you can't lead them into a change of heart. You must accept that the person does not care and is not interested. You must find an open window. You cannot force the other person to feel the same as you. If the person does not care about your goal, they do not need to be around you. It creates an imbalance that will break apart a family, work relationship, marriage, or friendship. The person will be unhappy, dissatisfied and resentful that you are imposing your will on them. They will throw tantrums, sabotage work, whine, complain, not show up and overall be miserable.

You can identify those that share your passion by looking for their interest when you speak about your goals. Look for a sparkle in the corner of their eye or an intent stare as you speak. The person may come closer or lean into you as you are talking. These are clear signs of interest. The motivation must come from a deep hunger in your spirit. While it's easy to fake enthusiasm, it's harder to fake passion. You cannot journey together with anyone who does not have passion or fortitude for what you are going to do.

Just as constant arguments and constant drama distract inspired people from reaching their goals, on the flip side, a true partnership will push you into your rightful destiny. Remember that every decision you make matters. Choose to walk with those that will help you reach your purpose. There is no need to go out and try to find people who have the same goals and passions. People will come and go in your life; you do not need to search for anyone. God will send the right people to you, it's your job to evaluate the relationship and know who they are. Find your open windows.

CHAPTER GEMS

- Confrontation allows you to see who people are clearly.
- We must be vulnerable and open to recognizing the truth.
- Don't put a band-aid on matters, face them with courage.
- You must be open, willing, and put yourself in the other person's shoes. Put your pride aside.
- When we become stubborn and immovable, we become stagnant.
- Give your attention to the word of God and focus on the things that matter.
- It's important to join with people who share your same passion and want the same objective.
- Most people will tell you who they are if you are willing to listen.
- When you don't listen to people, you may find yourself in energy draining relationships that can last for a lifetime.
- God will send the right people to you; it's your job to evaluate the relationship and know who they are.

YOUR GEMS

(How can you use the lessons in this chapter in your life? Use this page to write down your ideas, and insights.)

CHAPTER FOUR

Joys and Pains

In life we will experience joys, pains, challenges, sorrows and most importantly changes. We will see countless sunsets and take millions of deep breaths. We will experience life until our journey comes to an end. Life is short. We must place value on every second, minute and hour. Our time is precious and must not be wasted. It does not matter how wealthy, powerful, gorgeous or affluent you are; time is fleeting, and it waits for no one. When you understand the value of time, you make different decisions. You approach life, love, work, and even play differently. You understand that every moment counts.

When you repeat old mistakes, you waste your precious time. I understand that we will all make mistakes. Don't beat yourself up over mistakes you made in the past. The issue becomes when you keep doing the same things and expecting a different result. You cannot ride the same rollercoaster and think you're going to get a different ride. If something is not working for you, it's counterproductive to give your energy in the same way. Be adaptable to change and make effective use of your time.

Life is a journey not a race. You can run your race at your own pace but trust and enjoy the journey. Understand there are times in life you will feel happy and there are times you will feel sad. You may be angry one day and frustrated the next. Then another day you may be laughing and crying. No matter the ups or downs you are experiencing right now, enjoy your life. You only have one life, and these are your moments. Cherish them. Don't spend time worrying about things you cannot change and looking back to see who was left behind. Direct your attention to ensuring you have what you need to live your best life now. Take one step at a time but keep stepping. Sadly, it took Corrine quite some time to learn this lesson.

Intimate Partner Violence

Intimate partner violence is usually motivated by the desire to have and maintain power over one's partner. It can be in the form of emotional or physical abuse or both. Corinne's intimate partner violence started off with Travis mushing her in the face. Travis explained he was just being playful. Then it changed to constant and full on beatings.

Once Corinne and Travis got into a petty argument that led to him going into a rage. He grabbed Corinne by the throat with one hand and began punching her in the face and body with the other hand. Travis attempted to drag Corinne out of the house, telling her he intended to kill her in the woods just outside the house. Corinne screamed for help at the top of her lungs, but it seemed no one either heard her or just didn't want to be involved. He ripped all of Corinne's clothes off, grabbed her by her hair, and drug her on the harsh blue carpet towards the front door of the house. Corinne grabbed the door frame trying to slow him down. Clouded by pain, Corinne started to tell him how much she loved him and that she only wanted to be with him. Travis suddenly picked her up off the floor and grabbed her again by her neck. "You love me, Corinne?" Travis's steely grey eyed scoured Corinne's looking for her sincerity. "Baby, I love you," Corinne sputtered in between gasps for air. Travis let go of his grip on Corinne's neck and dropped her to the floor. He looked at Corinne intensely for a few seconds and walked out the front door. That incident should have caused Corrine to re-evaluate her life, and approach it differently. It didn't.

Corinne's body crumbled as she lay there sobbing. Travis's anger had once again caught her off guard. She had no clue what would set him off. Her head and body felt like they were on fire. Corinne slowly made her way to the bathroom mirror and recoiled in shock at what she saw. Her face was disfigured because of the swelling. She could barely open her mouth. Her eyes were swollen and barely able to stay open. Corinne cried through her pain. She knew she had to get away from Travis and she could only think of one place to go.

She took her son and decided to make the hour long walk to her parent's house. Corinne walked through the night looking up at the stars periodically. She wanted to wish her problems away. At around 1 a.m., Corinne arrived at her parent's house, knocked on the door and rang the doorbell. She needed help and she had nowhere else to go; Corinne just knew her parents would help her.

Harold opened the door and looked at Corinne's face in disgust.

"What do you want, Corinne?" Her father asked coldly.

"I want to come home," Corinne mumbled through her swollen mouth, which was making it increasingly difficult for her to speak. He looked at his bruised and broken daughter standing before him asking him for help and felt no compassion.

He paused and coolly stated, "Corinne, you can't come back in this house. You would be a distraction for the other kids and I cannot have that. The only thing I can offer you and your bastard son is that you sleep in one of our cars in the driveway."

Corinne couldn't believe her ears. "I need help, Daddy" Corinne cried. She repeatedly asked him for help hoping somehow Harold would understand her despair.

"Corinne, I'm tired. Make a decision so I can go back to sleep!" He didn't try to hide his disdain.

Corinne's pain and despair turned to anger. Her family never had her back, she thought. "Never mind."

Her response prompted Harold to abruptly slam the door in Corinne and Sean's faces. Corinne was floored at her father's response. She swallowed her tears and walked back to more of Travis's abuse. She was out of options.

Over time, Travis's family would witness the abuse, but they never intervened. One day Travis's aunt and uncle were taking her and Travis to the store. Travis's uncle was driving, and his aunt was in the front passenger's seat. Travis, Corinne, and baby Sean were in the backseat. They all went into the store and were headed back to the vehicle when a car playing loud music drove by Corinne slowly. Corinne looked towards the car, which threw Travis in a rage. Suddenly, Travis smacked the back of Corinne's head hard.

"Get in the car! Oh, you know that dude, Corinne1 Don't try to play me, get in the damn car!"

"Travis, I don't . . ."

"Get in the damn car!"

The abuse continued for the duration of the car ride. Corinne asked Travis's aunt and uncle to pull over and get Travis off her, but they refused. Travis's uncle said they needed to work out their issues, all while watching Travis punch Corinne mercilessly. Corinne knew she would have to fight this battle alone and it would not be the first or last time.

Their love/hate relationship had taken her through so much these past years. Every time she got away from Travis, he found a way to pull her back in. He always told her that the two of them were family, and sometimes families fight. Travis would bring Corinne in close to him and whisper to her how things would get better and that he would change. Corinne somehow knew that Travis wouldn't change but she prayed he would. They had a son and she wanted to have her family together.

Another time, after Travis, Corinne, and Sean moved into their own apartment, Travis grabbed Corrine and forcefully threw her through the double glass window in their bedroom. Travis watched the aftermath of his actions in horror. He never wanted to hurt Corinne. It was as if Corinne was going through the window in slow motion. Travis's hard push into the glass caused it to explode all around them. Corinne moved out of the broken windowsill just as the jagged glass hanging from the top of the window frame slammed down, narrowly missing Corinne's neck. It was at that moment she knew her time with Travis was over. Corinne heard Travis apologizing through his sobs. She felt sorry for Travis because she knew he didn't mean to act so irrationally. But she felt even worse for her son who witnessed the horrific abuse. Corinne knew it was time to make her escape. She was just unsure what to do.

Throughout her abusive relationship, Corrine managed to stay in touch with Kristen, Travis's cousin and Corrine's best friend. She waited for Travis to leave the apartment that fateful night and when he did, she called Kristen to ask for her help. Thankfully, Kristen came through.

It can be challenging to figure out where a situation may rank in matters of importance. For Corrine, finding a safe place for her son and herself became her priority. Life was teaching her that she could no longer waste her time on Travis and her hopes that she would have the family she wanted. It was time to sift through each situation in her life:

an abusive relationship, being a 16-year-old mother of a 2-year-old, no support from hers or Travis's family, and no way to take care of herself and her son.

Figuring Out What's Important

We spend so much time on things that are not important. We only have a certain amount of resources and we can't waste them. Corrine wasted years of her life which led to her suffering. One of the worst things you can do is waste time. It is a precious commodity that needs to be respected.

There is a popular saying that you must lose to win. This means you must get rid of old relationships, fears, practices, and guilt. Life is tough, and we go through so much as it is. Don't add unnecessary stress into your life. When you come to the realization that you can avoid some bad times, you should pay attention. Don't complicate your life by refusing to leave behind what no longer serves you. You are greater than those things. Don't waste your precious time just to entertain a bad time. As a young mother, you probably want the father of your child to be in your life. Maybe you feel like Corrine, and you're in an abusive relationship—all in the name of family.

Prayer can help us focus on what is important and what isn't. Ask God to determine what to keep in your life and what to release. It's not always easy to figure out what to keep and what to let go. You need the wisdom and clarity that only the Infinite Spirit brings. Ask God to show you what enhances energizes, enables, and motivates you. Ask him to reveal what depletes, defeats and drains you. He will lead you to clarity.

Learn How to Let Go

There is a show on T.V. called "Hoarders." In this show you see people who can't use the basic functions of the house because they have so much clutter around. I watched a show where a woman could not get into her bathroom because of the mess she had around the door. She was going to the bathroom in a bucket. When her family came to help her remove the junk she had acquired, she fought and threw a huge temper tantrum. The woman was blind to the benefits of throwing away the clutter, like being able sit on an actual toilet seat. The woman couldn't muster up the inner strength to act on her own behalf. She was a victim of her own self-sabotage.

"Hoarders" went on for many seasons and it opened people's eyes to the fact that some seemingly normal people were living in unique living situations. So many people keep old things that need to be thrown away. We are loyal to what feels familiar but offers nothing else. It's a waste of your time to be loyal to things that are not loyal to you. Corrine needed to find the courage to let her abusive relationship with Travis go; you must have the courage to let things go. You have options and it's time you recognize that. You are the prize. When you get rid of the unnecessary junk, you will open to see what lies ahead. The choice is yours, so don't be too lazy or afraid to use it.

The Power of Choice

Make a list of the pros and cons of each choice. You cannot win it all and you won't lose it all. You must find balance. There will be assets and liabilities, but don't let that dampen your spirit. You hold the power of choice. Make the decision as to what you will allow and what you will not. Your spirit cannot be weighed down by unnecessary influences. You must keep your channels of creativity open and prioritize accordingly. There are some things you will have to hold on to and others you can throw in the trash immediately. You can make room for some troubles, but others should not be your concern. Focus on developing your priorities, making sound decisions and bringing closure to what no longer serves you. Remember, you are not meant to hold on to stinky trash.

You cannot receive the new, holding on to the old. You must release the fear that you will be in a state of lack. God will always provide. Trust in Him. Fear makes us incapable of making clear decisions. Fear clutters our minds and paralyzes us. Fear will make us second guess ourselves and render us ineffective. We often are afraid that we are not good enough or are not going to reach the success we want to achieve. We tear ourselves down with baseless insecurities. We tell ourselves we are not pretty enough to achieve a certain this or smart enough to accomplish that. We tear ourselves down before we have a chance to begin. We must keep in mind that we are God's children and we are made to be great. There is no person below us or above us. We are successful because we are His.

CHAPTER GEMS

- When you repeat old mistakes, you waste your precious time.
- Don't spend time worrying about things you cannot change and looking back to see who was left behind.
- It can be challenging to figure out where a situation may rank in matter of importance.
- Don't complicate your life by refusing to leave behind what no longer serves you.
- Ask God to show you what enhances energizes, enables, and motivates you.
- When you get rid of the unnecessary junk, you will open to see what lies ahead.
- You hold the power of choice.
- You cannot receive the new, holding on to the old.
- Keep in mind that you are God's child and you were made to be great. There is no person below you or above you. You are successful because you are His.

YOUR GEMS

(How can you use the lessons in this chapter in your life? Use this page to write down your ideas, and insights.)

CHAPTER FIVE

Passing the Test

"You have no other options." Reluctantly, Corrine accepted the truth of those five words and their impact on her life. By this time, she was 16 years old and pregnant for the second time. Corrine realized that she had to make a life for herself and her children—a life free of Travis and the constant physical and emotional abuse.

Teen mothers are likely to have a second birth which can further inhibit their ability to finish school or keep a job. About one-fourth of teenage mothers have a second child within 24 months of the first birth[5].

At Kristen's urging, she left Travis and went to Social Services for help. Despite problems associated with Corrine's

[5] Teen Birth Article

young age, the social worker was able to place her and Sean into a shelter and later helped her get her first apartment.

Some moments truly test us. Faced with the chance to escape from an abusive relationship without knowing where she and Sean would end up was one of those moments for Corrine. No doubt she felt like she couldn't handle the situation and was fearful that she wouldn't make it through. We tell ourselves we will not make it and speak death into our goals. We have put down the armor of God and replaced it with cardboard. We work against ourselves and lessen our effectiveness. We let insecurity turn into a self-created plague. Our tongues must be used in praise and positivity, not to throw up ash and speak negativity. We have the power within us to command greatness. We must speak life into ourselves.

There will be real issues you have to deal with and real enemies to battle in life. In fact, Jeannine Amber writes, "For many teenagers the path from pregnancy to successful parenting is riddled with what feels like insurmountable obstacles. They must quickly learn to provide and care for their children, figure out how to continue their education, secure employment, and possibly housing, all while negotiating their journey through adolescence." Don't weigh yourself down with imaginary issues. When you try your best at something, that is all you can do. Let the rest go. If you don't win first place in a race, it's okay if you know you tried your best. Trying your best is what counts. Don't beat yourself up over things you tried your best on. It's silly and futile. You are creating feelings of doubt and regret within yourself for no reason. Stop it! When you focus on regret, you will not only feel terrible, you will lose trust in yourself. You will feel despair and it will cause you to doubt your abilities. You do not deserve to suffer at your own hands.

Your highest priority should be to get rid of the fear binding your life. When you get up in the morning and look in the mirror, tell yourself how beautiful, gifted and courageous you are. Tell yourself how loving and wonderful you are. Wrap your arms around yourself and give yourself a big hug. You are amazing. When you tell yourself how much you hate your (fill in the blank), you are hating yourself. The truth is this: you are a beautiful, purpose-driven child of God. You deserve to hear loving words. You must honor yourself if you want to reach your full potential.

Faith or Fear

Fear is the opposite of faith. Fear is useless and the longer you hold on to it, the stronger its grip on your life. Teen parents hear negative messages around them all the time. While in the shelter, Corrine met a young woman who would help her overcome her fears. Jayda was a four feet, eleven-inch power house. Her gentle spirit seemed to radiate every time she spoke.

Jayda

Jayda told Corinne she wanted to help teach her about life. This time, Corinne finally had the sense to listen. Corinne was at a pivotal moment in her life. She was looking for direction and knowledge on how to improve her current situation and so was Jayda. The difference was Jayda had a unique perspective to handling life's challenges while Corrine had yet to develop a perspective on how to handle life's challenges. After Jayda shared her story with Corinne, Corinne instantly respected her.

Jayda was born to a mother unable to deal with her birth because her father, a married man, refused to leave his wife once he found out Jayda's mother was pregnant. Her mother, Lisa, lost all touch with reality and began to physically abuse young Jayda. After her father witnessed cigarette burns and bruises on his daughter, he had her placed in the home of his Uncle Lyle and Lyle's wife Shannon. Lyle was a pedophile who repeatedly raped 12-year-old Jayda impregnating her. Distraught, Jayda tried unsuccessfully to abort Lyle's child by using a twisted wire clothes hanger. She then told her Aunt Shannon who flew into a rage and nearly beat Jayda to death, accusing her of tempting Lyle until he could no longer control himself. Jayda gave birth and gave the child to Lyle and Shannon to raise. Corinne felt so sorry for Jayda. She wondered how she was still standing. Jayda was a like a beacon of hope to Corinne.

It's amazing how others can inspire you by sharing their pain. Before Jayda's arrival, Corinne wasn't doing too well at the shelter. She was going through an extreme sense of loneliness and abandonment. Leaving Travis had taken its toll on Corinne. She dreamed of Travis and had nightmares of her father. Corinne desperately needed someone like Jayda in her life and she never knew how much until Jayda arrived. Jayda made it her mission to be a good example for Corinne. She became a hybrid of big sister mixed with mentor for Corinne.

Jayda would create made-up dilemmas for Corinne to strategize. She would ask Corinne to write down the pros and cons, prior to making any decision on what to do. Jayda told Corinne she could achieve anything her mind could conceive. Jayda was a good friend to Corinne who added value to her life. She taught Corrine how words fuel fear and become buried into your subconscious mind.

The Three Areas of the Mind

Experts tell us that we think from three areas of the mind: the subconscious mind, the conscious, and the superconscious. All three must work together in harmony to achieve balance in your life.

Conscious

- *Conscious mind is awareness.*
- *The conscious mind is simply where our attention is at the moment.*
- *With conscious awareness, we are able to make changes.*
- *Our abilities lie in what we are aware of—thinking analytically, logical order, conscious choices, asking why and coming up with solutions based on fact.*

Subconscious

- *It is where our emotions, memories, and beliefs are.*
- *It is the power of the mind in sending electrical impulses of information to billions of cells in our body.*
- *And it decodes the imagination, the feelings, the impulses, sensations, and instincts which results in intuition, deep insights and wisdom.*

- *In changing our subjective world, we create a different experience in the outer reality.*

Superconscious

- *Our superconscious mind is the awareness that sees the subjective and objective reality, and even beyond.*
- *It is also known as Higher Self or Higher Mind.*
- *We receive our intuition, inspiration, and sense of morality and wisdom from our superconscious mind.*[6]

Releasing Fear

When we hear negative words and images they embed themselves into our conscious mind and we act on those negative images and words. We no longer need to see or hear the negativity because we have allowed its weeds to take root. We clip our own wings causing fear to manifest itself in different ways. Fear will make you feel like you have the weight of the world sitting on your shoulders. Fear can show itself through petty actions and unfocused anger. Fear can fuel you to be an overachiever because you have a point to prove. Fear affects your character and how you perceive others. It can mask your conscious mind to what is right and what is wrong.

When you are fearful, you do deceitful things to get ahead. You create fights when there is no fight. When you are fearful, you sabotage your co-workers project or your teammates' performance. You step on another person's back to climb the ladder of success. There is a difference between success and good success. Good success doesn't cause another

---

[6] http://2empowerthyself.com/the-trinity-of-mind-the-conscious-subconscious-and-unconscious-mind

sorrow; it makes you feel good about yourself. You did the hard work and it payed off. When you simply have success, it is unfulfilling and lonely. You made it to the top, but at what cost? Make sure you aim to achieve "good" success.

To tackle fear head on you need to study yourself and identify your motives. Fear will hide your true motivations with emotions like anger and strife. Keep it real with yourself and don't hide your true feelings. There is no need to lie to yourself. God is here to protect and empower you to look within your heart. The Infinite Spirit is here to defend you. All you need to do is trust Him.

Keep questioning every day how you can lighten your load. You can't move into greatness carrying an overflowing trash bag. Garbage has no place in your life as it weighs you down. You have so much to look forward to. Stay focused on reaching the top of the mountain. God wants us to desire Him and He want His word to motivate us. He speaks to us, if only we will listen. We must be courageous in the face of our fears. When old issues arise, you must be ready and willing to say goodbye to those that keep you in the same place. Don't let old issues hold you hostage. God has given us the key to our freedom, we must be willing to place our key in the lock and turn it. Be brave enough to identify your fears and the courage to release them into the wind so you can soar to your highest of heights.

CHAPTER GEMS

- You have the power within you to command greatness.
- Don't weigh yourself down with imaginary issues.
- You are a beautiful, purpose-driven child of God.
- Fear is useless. The longer you hold on to fear, the stronger its grip on your life.
- You can achieve anything your mind can conceive.
- Words fuel fear and become buried in your subconscious mind: watch what you say to yourself.
- There is a difference between success and good success. Good success makes you feel good about yourself, while simple success leaves you unfulfilled and lonely.
- Study yourself and your motives.
- Don't let old issues hold you hostage.
- God has given you the key to your freedom, you must be willing to put the key in the lock and turn it.

YOUR GEMS

(How can you use the lessons in this chapter in your life? Use this page to write down your ideas, and insights.)

CHAPTER SIX

Bogus Commitments

A bogus commitment is one that attaches itself to you because someone helped you out and now they feel like you owe them. These seemingly innocent debts quickly become heavy burdens. Jacob was Corrine's bogus commitment.

It was an uneventful Monday for Corinne the day she met Jacob. She was exhausted, pregnant and at work. She welcomed her lunch break to step outside. She had no money for lunch, but she just needed the fresh air.

"You are so beautiful."

"Thank you."

"Where are you off to, Beautiful?"

"I'm just taking a walk," Corrine said in her sweetest voice.

"Well, I'm about to grab some food if you want to join me, it's my treat."

"Sure," mentally allowing her hunger to overrule her apprehension. She felt like she should know better than to go someplace with a new guy, but the reality was she was pregnant; she needed to eat.

Jacob and Corinne shared stimulating conversation while eating lunch. She learned that he believed in the power of education and was also heavily involved in the community. He provided mentorship for students after school and worked as a bus driver during the day. He seemed like an all-around great guy. Jacob listened to Corinne tell a bit of her story and he stopped her and said, "this is our story now." Corinne asked Jacob what he meant by that.

"It's you and me now and forever."

Corinne laughed. "Aren't you going to ask me how I feel first?"

"I don't have to ask you; your heart is already speaking to me"

Corinne was a sucker for a good looking, charming man. But she was pregnant, and he needed to know that.

"Jacob, I'm pregnant." Corinne blurted out.

"I know; it's no secret." Jacob stated with a half laugh.

"So, what do you want with me, Jacob?"

"I want us."

"Just like that?"

"Just like that," Jacob replied as he stared deeply in her eyes and smiled.

From then on it was Corinne and Jacob. Their relationship moved fast, and it seemed like it was perfect timing in a lot of ways. Still reeling from the sudden death of her dear friend and mentor, Jayda, Corrine was vulnerable to Jacob's show of kindness, concern, and love.

Corinne's one-year lease would be up before she knew it and she had a small child plus a new baby on the way. Jacob seemed to need to know every shred of Corinne's business. He was a few years older than Corinne and he said he was in her life to help her. He even moved her and Sean into a bigger apartment.

Pay Attention

Life with Jacob was peaceful. She no longer needed to work, and she loved being in Jacob's presence. He was sweet and kind to her and Sean. He made her forget all that she went through with Travis.

Once Tyler, her second child, was born Jacob slowly started to change. Immediately, Jacob began to tell everyone that Tyler was his biological son, which made Corinne feel uneasy since Tyler and Jacob looked nothing alike. It began to look as if Corinne had tricked Jacob into thinking that Tyler was his baby. Corinne approached Jacob with her concerns.

"Baby, I don't understand why you keep telling people Tyler is yours. People are starting to look at me like I fooled you."

Jacob's face recoiled in pain. "So, Tyler isn't my baby?

"Yes, he is your baby, but you know he is not *your* baby." Corinne emphasized.

"Corinne, I'm doing all this for you. You don't think it hurts me to walk out of this hospital room with another man's son?"

"You knew all this before Jacob. Why are you trying to make me feel guilty?"

"Because you should!"

Later, Jacob moved his brother in with them who spent his days playing video games. His laziness seemed to wear off on Jacob. As time went on, Jacob started to stay out late drinking. He seemed to be moving backwards; he was missing days at work and even had her call out for him citing an emergency with the kids. Eventually, he quit his job because he was "tired of working." It was turning into a nightmare. Money in the house began to go missing.

Corrine felt like Jacob knew he held all the power and it wasn't a good feeling, but she felt obligated because of all he had done for her. She should have paid attention to the signs. Despite her misgivings, including the safe he brought into the house for no apparent reason, when he asked her to marry him, she agreed. However, on the day of the wedding, she found ultrasound pictures he had hidden in the safe—and they did not have her name on them. He had gotten someone else pregnant, and to make matters worse, Corrine was pregnant with her third child—Jacob's child. Clearly, Jacob had made a bogus commitment.

Misplaced Praise

Some people incite a feeling that you should forever be grateful to them. When someone does a favor for you, helping them out in return seems like the decent thing to do. A problem is created when we place that person on a pedestal for helping us. We make them feel like they are ever powerful, and we would be nothing without their assistance. We praise them and tell everyone how good they have been to us. We give the person the glory instead of God. We are suggesting our protection comes from a person and not from the Infinite Spirit.

Your protection comes from God. God sponsored your upgrade. As you traverse the rocky road of teenage parenthood, you must remember that it is God who strengthens you to make it. He is the worker of miracles, not man. God may use someone to get your foot in the door, but it is your gifts that will keep that door ajar. We cannot answer the ring of indentured servitude calling on us to serve everyone who shows us a dollop of kindness. Appreciate the help but lose the feeling of being in debt. You do not owe anyone anything just as no one owes you anything. Some people will do something nice for you and ride that good deed until the wheels fall off. They will bring up what they did for you every chance they get. You will be so sick and tired of hearing about what they did for you until you wish they never helped you in the first place. They will act like they were the sole reason for your success and you had better not forget it.

Make sure you give people what you owe them, so you are not weighed down with resentment, petty debts and imaginary offences. We cannot allow anyone to manipulate us into thinking we owe them for a lifetime as a show of gratitude. And there are some people have blessed us in ways we will always remember. We love, adore and appreciate them as we should, but there are some people who always want more than they are due. They destroy relationships out of their need for residual repayment. For example, once their daughter, Cara, was born, Jacob stopped paying the rent. Corinne had to make the choice of using her savings to pay off the eviction; or, use the money for a down payment on a new place.

Free Yourself from Make-Shift Bill Collectors

People who want more than they are due, ruin partnerships and relationships. They leave you feeling exhausted as you try to please them. You slowly realize no matter how many deeds you do for them, they expect more. The person feels the debt will never be settled. They do not realize the debt has already been settled and is paid in full. Don't allow these makeshift bill collectors to keep taking energy from you. You do not owe them a thing.

It's not easy to let go of these types of people. They act like leeches, trying to suck every ounce of blood out of you. These individuals want you to fly, but they want to control the height. If you fly too high without their permission, they will try to find a way to clip your wings. Keep in mind, there are no chains binding or holding you down. You must make the choice to soar and remove their noose from around your neck. They do not own you because they did something nice for you. You cannot please everyone, and you should not try. You are not a doormat, do not let people walk all over you.

You will run across those that take your kindness as a weakness. Be nice but do not be taken advantage of. Don't allow your niceness to overshadow your common sense. Do not keep putting others on a pedestal while you are being crushed by the weight of their obligations. You have already paid back the favor and now you must release the debt. Free yourself.

CHAPTER GEMS

- A bogus commitment is one that attaches itself to you because someone helped you out and now they feel like you owe them. These seemingly innocent debts quickly become heavy burdens.
- Remember, God sponsored your upgrade. Give Him the praise.
- God may use someone to get your foot in the door, but it is your gifts that will keep that door ajar.
- Appreciate the help but lose the feeling of being in debt.
- We cannot allow anyone to manipulate us into thinking we owe them for a lifetime as a show of gratitude.
- There are some people who always want more than they are due. They destroy relationships out of their need for residual repayment.
- There are no chains binding or holding you down. You must make the choice to soar.
- You cannot please everyone, and you should not try.
- You are not a doormat, do not let people walk all over you.
- You have already paid back the favor and now you must release the debt. Free yourself.

YOUR GEMS

(How can you use the lessons in this chapter in your life? Use this page to write down your ideas, and insights.)

CHAPTER SEVEN

Confront and Release

"One of the unspoken tragedies for many teen parents is the loss of faith that a bright future is theirs. Before they became pregnant, many young mothers had been planning for life beyond high school. But with the arrival of a child, *(and in Corrine's case, three children)* their focus turns to fulfilling their most immediate needs—securing diapers, formula and clothes. Meanwhile, the important task of setting goals and creating a long-term plan for success falls by the wayside."[7] The only way to hold on to your dreams, especially as a teen parent, is to keep your goals in mind. You cannot allow familiarity or temporary comfort to overpower your judgment. Commit to making the most of your moments and make the hard choices necessary to live your best life.

[77] Engaging, Ensuring and Elevating: Essential Strategies for Mentoring Pregnant and Parenting Teens by Jeannine Amber

Seven Truths to Help You Confront and Release

1. Life isn't a fairytale; you will face disappointments.

   When we lie to ourselves, we set ourselves up for failure. We cannot cast reality aside. We must be real with ourselves regarding what is happening in our lives. If a certain relationship or thing is not working for you, despite your best efforts, admit it. Don't try to look at the relationship or thing through rose colored glasses. Stop lying to yourself and realize the relationship or thing has failed. You are trying to breathe life into what is already dead.

   Accept that even though you tried your very best, you cannot salvage it. You may feel a strong pull to keep working on the relationship or thing instead of cutting ties. In these moments, reflect on the fact you have no more to give. You have already tried your best. Take a deep breath, swallow your pride and release these dead situations and people to God. Let Him handle them and pray for improvement.

2. You can't be everything to everybody

   When we empathize with others, we naturally want to help. Many times, you can help. You will encounter people who will always need your help.

However, be cautious when someone is always calling on you for help and making you feel guilty if you can't help. Only God can help some people.

You cannot successfully walk through life carrying another person on your back. The weight of carrying the other person will eventually deplete you. You can loan a friend $20 once or twice, but when you're paying his rent, buying his clothes, and generally paying for his responsibilities, that's another thing. You become an enabler. Just as if you broke your leg and need crutches to lean on for support to walk, you have become the person's crutch. The person is neither motivated nor empowered to take control of their life. Why should they try when they have you there to do everything for them?

While it feels good to help others, it feels good to be needed sometimes. The problem occurs when your desire to feel needed conflicts with the other person's growth. Growth cannot occur when you are already doing the action for the person. You are stunting that person's growth. Let the person learn to do for themselves. They will be better off because you cannot always be around. It's God's job to teach this person, so get out of His way. Allow God to provide for this person and focus on what you need to do for yourself.

3. Get comfy with criticism

Perhaps you've decided to end a relationship. Do not be surprised if everyone is not happy about your decision. You cannot please everyone, and everyone cannot be pleased. That means simply, do not worry about what others think. What do you think? That is what matters. You cannot stress yourself as to what anyone will think of you or worry about what they will say. You know what you must do, and you cannot allow fear to dictate your actions.

People get very sensitive when it comes to ending a relationship. Some will be angry, bitter, resentful and hostile. They may strongly feel you are making the wrong decision by ending things. They may become jealous and feel like you are leaving them behind. They may try to retaliate by being petty or through anger. You just need to understand and accept that some people may not like your actions. You only have one life and you must be able to focus on your journey. You can't reach your true potential when you give energy to worry instead of preparation.

There will be times in your life where you will have to speak the truth. You will often find the truth hurts. There is a saying, coined by Alabama-born alcoholic-turned-Methodist-evangelist Samuel Porter

Jones that goes, "The hit dog will always holler." That means that a person who is offended by something someone has done will tell that person. When we tell our truth, we must be willing to accept the consequences. Some people will criticize you. When you do not speak the truth, you participate in a lie. You become a liar by default. When someone continually takes your kindness for a weakness and you do not speak up for yourself, you are telling a lie. It bothers you, so say that. Do not allow your discomfort to continue at the hands of another.

Even if the people are always praising you to others and telling others how much of a God-send you are in their lives. You don't need those compliments, they cost too much. Let them keep their compliments while you save your energy. You can't allow yourself to be knocked off your journey for the sake of anyone. You are far too important.

4. Teach people how to treat you

When you establish boundaries in the beginning of a relationship, you have higher chances of success. You may have heard the saying, "You teach people how to treat you." If you let people treat you in a way that makes you feel disrespected, taken advantage of or uncomfortable, what they take from that is you are okay with their behavior. We also must keep in mind our desire for privacy and space. It may only take one time for a person to feel like they can run all over you. Here are some examples of boundaries:

- Don't go through someone's purse, backpack, phone, computer, desk drawer, etc. If you want something from a place the person considers private, please ask .
- If the bathroom door is closed, please knock or wait. Don't just walk in.
- If you see something unusual in the kitchen, please respect the time and efforts enough to ask if it's for something special before you decide to help yourself.
- You might decide certain topics of conversation are off limits with some people. If so, tell them as soon as you think it's an issue.

Boundaries make people aware of the things that are important to you. One of the ways people show each other respect and kindness is by honoring those boundaries. It's a way to show consideration, love and care. Establishing boundaries helps to alleviate the hurt feelings, bruised egos and misunderstandings.

Develop your boundaries early to lessen the possibility of misunderstandings. You don't have time for extra drama on your journey to greatness. You must clearly state your boundaries and make sure both parties accept and understand their role. Don't be afraid to renegotiate your boundaries. Some boundaries may be working for you and some may not. You may even grow out of some of them and that is okay. Keep in mind if a person is not treating you fairly, now is always the right time to speak up.

5. Sort and define your relationships

Ask yourself how much time, effort and resources you are willing to devote to each relationship. You ultimately have control. You do not have to stick around when people drain you. If you feel physically and/or emotionally drained every time you see their number on your caller ID, you have probably devoted too much energy into the relationship. Some people require more energy than others, but you must determine how much you are willing to give. You only have a certain amount of energy, so you must figure out the best use of your time.

When people need a lot of energy from you to feel close to you, it's draining. It seems like every few minutes you receive a text from them and they expect you to respond back based on their time and even get upset if you don't respond back fast enough. They need you to do them a favor or to loan them some money. They call you all the time and expect you to spend all your free time with them. You feel overloaded with their needs. These people are needy and want too many forms of attention. If you like to be around someone who is needy, then that type of relationship is workable for you. On the other hand, if you cannot stand to be around needy people, then the relationship may not be best for you. Just know you do not have an obligation to keep giving. You set the tone for your relationships.

6. Gradually work to release dead relationships

You may have heard the saying "phasing out" relationships. This means to slowly decrease contact with someone with the intention to progressively end the relationship. Some relationships can become violent fast if you end them abruptly. Sometimes the best move is to ease out of the relationship to whereas there are no harsh feelings and things feel natural. In the meantime, lessen their access to you, decrease phone calls and texts. Give limited access to you on social media. Don't frequent places you know you will have to interact with the person. Find new interests to take your mind off the situation.

There is no need to gossip about the situation. You are on your journey to greatness and that relationship is no longer working in your life. People may put up a fight once they realize they are being phased out; however, do not let guilt change your decision.

7. Stand firm in your decision

Once you have made the decision to end the relationship, there is no need to keep revisiting and going over your decision. There may even be people in your life who bring up your decision to end the relationship and tell you to try again. Make sure you are certain you want the relationship to end. Make sure you have no reasonable doubts. It may take some time for you to give up on a person or thing and that is okay. Make the decision once and make sure it is final. Don't get trapped in a cycle of doubting your decisions when you know what you must do. Make your final decision and be done with the relationship or thing. You cannot allow other's feelings to sway your decision when you know what is best for you.

Gain control over your life. Lose what is slowing your down and stealing your peace. Be decisive and stand firm in your decision. You are on your journey into greatness and there is no time or energy to waste second guessing what you have already decided upon.

CHAPTER GEMS

- Life isn't a fairy tale; you will face disappointments.
- You can't be everything to everybody.
- Get comfy with criticism.
- Teach people how to treat you.
- Sort and define your relationships.
- Gradually work to release dead relationships.

YOUR GEMS

(How can you use the lessons in this chapter in your life? Use this page to write down your ideas, and insights.)

CHAPTER EIGHT

Periods of Solitude

I've never been too fond of long car rides and maybe that's because I remember the agony of having to go to the bathroom and my father not wanting to stop the car. I remember feeling helpless and wishing he would just take a quick pause, so I could feel relieved. Then, there were those moments I've been in the car with someone who was clearly exhausted from driving but would not pull the car over or get a hotel for the night to rest. I would suffer through the ride having to watch the person sporadically fall asleep at the wheel and I would have to try to keep them awake. If only they could see the value of taking a pause. A pause would alleviate so many issues and it would be in the best interest of everyone in the car.

In life it's important to know when to pause and when to go ahead with full speed. You must know when it's time to pause, regroup, and replenish your energy. As you journey into greatness you become accustomed to the challenges that lie in wait for you and tend to prepare. While it's imperative to prepare, it's also equally critical to take periodic breaks. When you take a moment for yourself and enjoy something other than the everyday challenges of life, you will renew your spirit. You will be able to see the value of your efforts and become more effective in the process. Once Corrine was on her own, she was able to see just how much she had accomplished: she had three children, a good job. She was even enrolled in college.

Quiet Moments

There are times in life when you will want time by yourself, and there is nothing wrong with feeling this way. You need quiet moments to revive you. The calm and peaceful energy that absolute silence can bring is rejuvenating to your spirit. Sometimes, we feel tired even after we have had a good night's rest. We are fatigued and burned out, our spirit feels heavy and weighed down. We feel drained and uninspired. While we may still be motivated to go through the motions of life, after a while we miss our passion. This feeling happens to the strongest of us, even when we feel it won't happen to us. Being burned out manifests itself in different ways. You can lash out in irrational anger, act out at school or work, feel disconnected and numb, and overall be miserable. We may think work, people or circumstances are the root of our misery but the only person we need to look at is ourselves.

We have been so focused and steadfast on our journey, that we didn't take a bathroom break. Okay, so maybe you found your way to the bathroom during this time, but you understand the point. You must take a pause and rest before you burn out and lose sight of what you have been fighting for. Plus, you want to enjoy your journey, not just get through it. Pressing pause and taking a moment to yourself is not only in your best interest, but in the best interest of everyone around you. This journey is challenging, you must know when it's time to rest. Take a break from time to time to restore yourself and be your most productive self.

Preserving your Peace

Taking periodic pauses helps you see your journey with clarity. When you are burned out you can only see what is in front of you and it's easy to misappropriate priorities and contribute to your own demise. You stop looking at life with a sparkle in your eye. Don't lose your sparkle, have a mental breakdown or start making careless errors because you don't recognize when it's time to take a break. When you don't pause, your mind will find a way to find relief. We develop a thirst for the wrong things. This great need for release manifests as bad habits, commonly called "vices." With no relief, you become needy for the things that will rob you of your greatness. You don't understand why you have picked up these bad habits and why sin is now running rampant in your life. You try to hide your sin behind your progress, but all that happens in the dark will slowly be uncovered. You have lost the very control you seek.

It is in the beauty of solitude where our minds can flourish. It's hard to maintain your focus when you are not rested and just going through the motions. In calm and tranquil moments, we can rest our spirit and allow our creative energy to flow. You cannot rush your journey so enjoy your moments along the way. It's okay to pause and recollect your thoughts.

There are many times we wear a mask to show others a more polished view of ourselves. We leave our real self on the shelf and we forget who we are inside. We feel disconnected, yet we're so focused on being in control that we slowly poison our spirit with deceit. You must be who you are and know it's okay to be honest and transparent with the people you trust. Don't suffer in silence. Just because you may look like you have it all together, doesn't mean that you do. You may seem like a superhero to some and take on an invincible type of energy. It's time to accept that fact you are not invincible and need care and rest just like everyone else. Only God is invincible.

Be Vulnerable

It's hard to be vulnerable and show our pain, especially when you have always been the person everyone leans on. People have forgotten you are human and you even feel like you're untouchable. Well, you are in for a hard and confusing fall if you don't stop for a moment and examine your motives. It's confusing because you have seemingly been able to do everything, and now you feel like your purpose is being questioned. You have been successful for so long that failure has not been an option. But what if you fail? God is there to nurture you back into balance!

You are more important than the work you do. Do not lie to yourself and make the work greater than your life. There is no need to sacrifice yourself for the cause. If your health fails because you have run yourself into the ground, no one wins. Allowing false pride to block your vulnerability sabotages your true greatness. You must know when it's time to rest, rethink and reenergize. You deserve to have a constant sparkle in your eye. There is no need to fail because you're tired and need rest. Tend to your soul.

Be Good to Yourself

Craft handwritten questions to yourself and after you read the question aloud, immediately write down the first answer that comes to mind. This exercise helps bring light to the people, places, situations or things that have your energy. If you don't work to actively identify the stress in your life, you will find yourself enduring bad times when you should be happy and smiling. Things will be going great outwardly but inwardly you will feel convicted. After all the hard work you have done to achieve success, you will feel empty instead of accomplished. It's not reasonable to think you're going to always feel amazing and motivated, there will be ups and downs on your journey. You will not always feel happy and there will be moments that will cause great stress and pain. However, continuous stress without rest, is not the way to a great journey.

What's Your Stress Level?

Take a pause and relish in all you have already achieved. To gauge your stress level, write a simple yes or no for the first part, and respond thoughtfully to the follow up questions:

1. Do you feel grumpy and have low energy when you are away from school or work? What do you think is causing you to feel this way?
2. Does your life feel monotonous and lack variety? What are you looking forward to in the next week?
3. When you wake up in the morning, do you feel exhausted and fatigued? Do you feel like it's hard to drag yourself out of your bed?
4. Do you feel like you are slowly losing your sense of humor, passion, desire or optimism?
5. When you accomplish one goal, do you take the time to reflect on your achievement or do you just jump to the next goal on your list?
6. Do you find yourself crying unexpectedly or feel a sense of inner hopelessness?
7. Are you defining yourself based on your accomplishments rather than who you are as a person?
8. Do you find yourself making careless mistakes and lowering your standards to things you were once particular about?
9. Are you clenching your jaws, clasping your hands in distress and feeling overwhelmed by problems that seem too hard to make sense of?

10. Is the person you portray in public conflicting with the person you are in private?

Take a tally of how many "yes" responses you have and if they equal more than six, you're burned out. You feel empty and uninspired. You are overloaded with responsibility and desperately need to attain balance. Obtaining balance is key. As I mentioned earlier, if we do not have balance, we will find vices to fill the voids. Our health can be adversely affected when we lack balance. We run the risk of drowning ourselves in our own despair when we lack proper rest. Relax, have a seat and pause. You will not miss anything that was meant for you. Your destination is and will always be towards greatness.

To relax your soul, you can do simple things like go to the park. You can take a walk barefoot in the grass, eat on one of the benches or just sit and watch nature in peace and quiet. Wake up early, make yourself a hot cup of tea and read an interesting book. Find simple ways to relax and escape the demands of life. I know today everyone expects you to be chained to your phone. Keep in mind that you do not always have to be available to people, it's quite alright to take time to yourself.

Allow Yourself Rest and Operate at Your Best

When you slow down and take a break it does not reflect negatively on you. You are still walking in your greatness. Allow yourself rest, so you can operate at your best. You can simultaneously like your life and need to take a break. Taking mini-vacations allows your mind to rest and you will find yourself happier in the long run. When you realize the world will go on with or without you, it may cause you to feel anxiety and panic. We may feel like we must run the race faster and go harder to reach our goals. It is during these moments when you must discover your own pace. The world does not define you; you define the world.

Achieving Balance

When we do the right thing at the right time, we achieve balance. Balance is not easy to attain but it is possible. If you are tossing and turning all night about a problem that can't be solved in the middle of night, you are out of alignment and need balance. In 1 Peter 5:7, God instructs us to cast our cares on Him. For many years I struggled with anxiety. I would stress to a point where my health was suffering. My nerves were frayed, and I had trouble picking up an object without my hands shaking. I had to come to the realization I was allowing what I had no control over to control me. I was letting my fears take over my life. It was only when I began to do what God called me to do, that I was able to achieve balance in my health. No longer do I focus on my fears. God makes all things new. You can achieve.

Time Is on Your Side

When you say you have had enough and need to rest, some people will put up a fight. They may feel like they know what you need, and rest is not it. Do not allow anyone to determine when you need to rest. You know when you need a break. Do not allow anyone to make you feel guilty for needing time away. You must take charge of your time and rest when you need to.

Sit Down

I stated earlier in the book that each level will demand a different you. This holds true for each chapter of your life. As you move into your next chapter, you need to rest in between. While you may not be ready to retire, you still have worked hard to make it to your new season. Have a seat and take a break; you deserve it.

What is Important?

Focusing on our goals can become an all engulfing personal mission. We work so hard to make sure we are at our best. We become so good at the work we are doing, it begins to consume all our time. We work when we know we should be resting. Being an overachiever is great if it doesn't lead to burn out. You can become so addicted to working and the accolades it brings, you lose sight of why you started in the first place. God does not want your health to suffer. Make sure your work is God inspired and rest when you need to. It's much harder to reach your goals when you are constantly running off fumes. Slowly wean yourself off your fast track lifestyle and refocus your efforts on your well-being. Take the time you need to rest so you can be at your best.

God wants us to enjoy the journey and not just the destination. Take the time to reward yourself for all your hard work. As a child, I faithfully entered the library's summer reading challenge. In the challenge, I was part of a team and was to read 100 books by the end of the summer to get a pizza party. My team usually won so we always enjoyed a delicious pizza party. I remember the pizza melting in my mouth. It seemed to taste better because it was in the form of a prize. It felt good to be rewarded for reaching my goal.

We all enjoy a reward at the end of a challenge. Having a prize helps motivate us towards our goal. Prizes should always have rest built in. Resting can be as simple as taking a long bike ride or soaking in a bubble bath. No matter the prize you pick, always remember you are the ultimate prize.

CHAPTER GEMS

- When you take a moment to yourself and enjoy something other than the everyday challenges of life, you will renew your spirit.
- You must take a pause and rest before you burn out and lose sight of what you have been fighting for.
- It is in the beauty of solitude where our minds can flourish.
- You cannot rush your journey so enjoy your moments along the way. It's okay to pause and recollect your thoughts.
- You are not invincible and need care and rest just like everyone else. Only God is invincible.
- You are more important than the work you do.
- Allowing false pride to block your vulnerability sabotages your true greatness.
- Continuous stress without rest, is not the way to a great journey.
- Find simple ways to relax and escape the demands of life.
- The world does not define you. You define the world.
- Do not allow anyone to determine when you need to rest.
- Take time to reward yourself for all your hard work.
- Remember, you are the ultimate prize.

YOUR GEMS

(How can you use the lessons in this chapter in your life? Use this page to write down your ideas, and insights.)

CHAPTER NINE

Developing a Life Plan

As we walk through life it's important to remember God has given us a map for our lives through the Bible. His word is filled with clear and hidden messages. We must take God's word and use it as a foundation to build our life plan. If we do not have a life plan, we will just be trying to make it through the day. We will walk through life reacting to its challenges, instead of being able to flow with life's ups and downs. You need to develop a life plan, Jewelz!

It is imperative you have a life plan. Just because you walk by faith does not mean you do not need a plan. God will do His part, but you must do yours. James 2:20 says, faith without works is dead. This means you need to have a working strategy as to how to accomplish your goals. When you have a limited plan, you manifest a limited vision. You need to create an ongoing and detailed vision for your success. If you want unlimited success, you need a limitless vision.

It can take years of planning, collaboration, patience and persistence before a goal is reached. While you are trekking the arduous journey towards greatness you are going to need to pack discipline, desire and determination. You need to consistently balance your action and energy around your goals. God wants you to thrive, not just survive. Make sure you reach for the stars when creating your plan.

You may be presented with many good opportunities in life and you will have to be selective about what you choose to do. Take the advice Jayda gave Corrine shortly after they met, write out the pros and cons of each opportunity to your decision making. Consider the time and energy that is required for each opportunity and consider your desired outcome. Some opportunities will work for you now and others may work in the future. Focus on what will work for you now. Make sure the desired outcome outweighs the risk. Ensure the opportunity is aligned with your life plan.

When you find an opportunity that aligns with your life plan, you need to have confidence that your plan will succeed. Having faith is the key to your success. What you think, you become. Believe you can, and you will. This does not mean go to a sea and ask God to turn water into wine, this means have faith that when you pray for a goal, God will give you direction. God is waiting to lead you, all you must do is ask.

If you do not have a plan, you have nothing to look forward to. There is a saying that if you do not know where you will be at in five years, you're already there. Not having a plan means you are just surviving and not living in your greatness.

You must find an objective to strive for. If you are looking for a direction, go to God in prayer. Keep in mind God is not going to show up in a puff of smoke. He usually sends us messages through His people. He wants us to flourish and that requires us to plan.

It takes courage, motivation and focus to activate your plan. Courage is needed to be decisive. You cannot spend countless years trying to figure out what path to take, you must decide. To make informed decisions, make sure you have the right information. You can make a more informed decision when you have all the data. Be surrounded by people who are experts in their field and do not waste your time with people who will waste your time with bad information.

You need wise and competent people giving you counsel. Keep in mind that just because a person has education, does not make them an expert in a field. You can have all the information, but the ultimate decision is yours. It's important to make your own decision because you are the one who must live with the consequences.

To make an informed decision requires you to research every possible outcome. Gather information from several sources but do not immediately act on them. Separate good information from bad information as you move along this process. Do not go with the first information rather evaluate all the information to make an informed decision.

As you uncover new sources of information you will come across many smart people. You will also run across smart, aggressive, and persuasive people. Do not be swayed by someone's aggressive behavior, this is your decision so take your time. You must determine your next move. Ask questions, get other opinions and make sure you study all information found. When you have all the facts, then you can make a confident decision.

Uncomfortably Comfortable

When looking for solid counsel, it's important to find the expert or "best knower." This expert may not currently be in your social circle, but it's important to seek people out when they have information that will help you. Social media makes connecting to experts much easier. Connect with people who respectfully challenge your views and strengthen your critical thinking skills. Surround yourself with those that stretch you and facilitate healthy growth. Immerse yourself in knowledge and step out of your comfort zone, doing so will help you to flourish spiritually, emotionally, and financially. To step into your greatness, remember:

1. Have a plan
2. Make decisions
3. Gather data
4. Be courageous enough to step outside your comfort zone.

The most important step is number four. You cannot live in indecision and fear; it's time to make a move. Set a goal and charter a path for yourself. You are not building your life from wavering luck. You are building a strong foundation based off solid information and God's loving guidance. It is time to act and claim your blessings. Your blessings are God's investments in you. God sees what we do and that is important to Him. God does not bless your feelings and thought process, he is looking at your works—your actions.

Prayer alone is not enough to sustain you on your journey. While prayer may release the favor of God, it is our actions which releases man's power. It is not enough to pray for a better relationship with your loved one. You must work to restore the relationship. It is not acceptable to simply pray for good grades. It is you that must gather data, study, and do the work. Relying on prayer alone is not what God wants. As I stated earlier, faith without works is dead. You must act, and prayer will enhance your efforts, but it is not meant to take its place.

When you consistently strive towards your purpose, you will begin to see supernatural doors open for you. As God's gifts begin to flourish within you, know they are for you and no one's else. There is no one who can do what you do. People can and will try to imitate you but will fail miserably. You are one of a kind. No one can match your energy, vision or determination. Take your gifts to God in prayer and ask Him to direct your steps.

Your gifts were given to you to fulfill His purpose. You may notice that God's gifts show up within us while struggling though life's challenges. As we pray, we must not miss God's response. He has implanted visions inside of each of us that present themselves through our dreams. Pay attention the subtle messages you receive from your surroundings.

Seek out others who share in your vision and passion, so you can further each other on your journey to greatness.

Greatness is Possible

I attended a Women's Conference a while back. The hostess announced, at the beginning of the conference, that the scheduled keynote speaker had a family emergency and was not able to make it. She assured us that the person filling in would not disappoint. I must admit I was a little irritated and considered leaving. I'm glad I didn't.

Imagine my surprise when my old neighbor, Corrine, was introduced as the keynote speaker. She was amazing. She talked about her journey as a teenage parent—all the ups and downs she endured to raise herself and three children. I will leave you with her sage advice: "Life will sometimes be hard. Reignite your deferred dreams You can, and you will overcome the hurdles that lay ahead. Greatness is possible."

CHAPTER GEMS

- It's important to remember God has given us a map for our lives through the Bible.
- Just because you walk by faith does not mean you do not need a plan.
- If you want unlimited success, you need a limitless vision.
- Focus on what will work for you now.
- When you find an opportunity that aligns with your life plan, have confidence that your plan will succeed.
- If you are looking for direction, go to God in prayer.
- It takes courage, motivation, and focus to activate your plan.
- You can make a better-informed decision when you have all the data.
- You need wise and competent people giving you counsel.
- To step into your greatness:
    - Have a plan
    - Make decisions
    - Gather data
    - Be courageous enough to step out of your comfort zone
- When you consistently strive towards your purpose, you will begin to see supernatural doors open for you.

- Take your gifts to God in prayer. Ask Him to direct your steps.
- Your gifts were given to you to fulfill God's purpose.
- Life will sometimes be hard.
- Reignite your deferred dreams.
- You can, and you will overcome the hurdles that lay ahead.
- Greatness is possible.

YOUR GEMS

(How can you use the lessons in this chapter in your life? Use this page to write down your ideas, and insights.)

Chapter Gems Compiled

Chapter 1: Enough

- Never rely on another person to drive you through life.
- You can only control yourself, no one else!
- People will keep dumping more and more into your cup if you do not speak up for yourself.
- For you to be your best self and complete the journey God has placed before you, it's imperative you take total control over your life.
- Take a stand and speak up for yourself. There is no fear in standing in your truth.
- Take full control of yourself so you can ascend to greatness.
- Your job is to be pleasing to God, not man.

- Use your God-given compass to decide the direction of your life.
- Focus on controlling yourself and following the plan God has for you.
- Learn how to let people know when you've had enough.

Chapter 2: Decisions and Consequences

- You must be able to identify which relationships work for you and which don't.
- You have real friends and fake friends. Separate yourself from the fake ones.
- Toxic relationships drain your energy, leaving you feeling hopeless.
- Despite the hell your parents may put you through, don't harden your heart towards them.
- Look for a spiritual mentor.
- Place yourself around people who want to see you win.
- Don't deal with drama when you do not have to.
- You must decide to let go of what is familiar to embrace the unfamiliar.
- Just because a person feels good to you, it does not mean they are good for you.
- People who cannot see your growth or your potential must be removed from your life.

Chapter 3: Fixed Windows

- Confrontation allows you to see who people are clearly.
- We must be vulnerable and open to recognizing the truth.
- Don't put band-aids on matters, face them with courage.
- You must be open, willing, and put yourself in the other person's shoes. Put your pride aside.
- When we become stubborn and immovable, we become stagnant.
- Give your attention to the word of God and focus on the things that matter.
- It's important to join with people who share your same passion and want the same objective.
- Most people will tell you who they are if you are willing to listen.
- When you don't listen to people, you may find yourself in energy draining relationships that can last a lifetime.
- God will send the right people to you; it's your job to evaluate the relationship and know who they are.
- Find your open windows.

Chapter 4: Joys and Pains

- When you repeat old mistakes, you waste your precious time.
- Don't spend time worrying about things you cannot change and looking back to see who was left behind.
- It can be challenging to figure out where a situation may rank in matter of importance.
- Don't complicate your life by refusing to leave behind what no longer serves you.
- Ask God to show you what enhances energizes, enables, and motivates you.
- When you get rid of the unnecessary junk, you will open to see what lies ahead.
- You hold the power of choice.
- You cannot receive the new, holding on to the old.
- Keep in mind that you are God's child and you were made to be great. There is no person below you or above you. You are successful because you are His.

Chapter 5: Passing the Test

- You have the power within you to command greatness.
- Don't weigh yourself down with imaginary issues.
- You are a beautiful, purpose-driven child of God.
- Fear is useless. The longer you hold on to fear, the stronger its grip on your life.

- You can achieve anything your mind can conceive.
- Words fuel fear and become buried in your subconscious mind: watch what you say to yourself.
- There is a difference between success and good success. Good success makes you feel good about yourself, while simple success leaves you unfulfilled and lonely.
- Study yourself and your motives.
- Don't let old issues hold you hostage.
- God has given you the key to your freedom, you must be willing to put the key in the lock and turn it.

Chapter 6: Bogus Commitments

- A bogus commitment is one that attaches itself to you because someone helped you out and now they feel like you owe them. These seemingly innocent debts quickly become heavy burdens.
- Remember, God sponsored your upgrade. Give Him the praise.
- God may use someone to get your foot in the door, but it is your gifts that will keep that door ajar.
- Appreciate the help but lose the feeling of being in debt.
- We cannot allow anyone to manipulate us into thinking we owe them for a lifetime as a show of gratitude.

- There are some people who always want more than they are due. They destroy relationships out of their need for residual repayment.
- There are no chains binding or holding you down. You must make the choice to soar.
- You cannot please everyone, and you should not try.
- You are not a doormat, do not let people walk all over you.
- You have already paid back the favor and now you must release the debt. Free yourself.

Chapter 7: Confront and Release

- Life isn't a fairy tale; you will face disappointments.
- You can't be everything to everybody.
- Get comfy with criticism.
- Teach people how to treat you.
- Sort and define your relationships.
- Gradually work to release dead relationships.

Chapter 8: Periods of Solitude

- When you take a moment to yourself and enjoy something other than the everyday challenges of life, you will renew your spirit.
- You must take a pause and rest before you burn out and lose sight of what you have been fighting for.
- It is in the beauty of solitude where our minds can flourish.
- You cannot rush your journey so enjoy your moments along the way. It's okay to pause and recollect your thoughts.
- You are not invincible and need care and rest just like everyone else. Only God is invincible.
- You are more important than the work you do.
- Allowing false pride to block your vulnerability sabotages your true greatness.
- Continuous stress without rest, is not the way to a great journey.
- Find simple ways to relax and escape the demands of life.
- The world does not define you. You define the world.
- Do not allow anyone to determine when you need to rest.
- Take time to reward yourself for all your hard work.
- Remember, you are the ultimate prize.

Chapter 9: Developing a Life Plan

- It's important to remember God has given us a map for our lives through the Bible.
- Just because you walk by faith does not mean you do not need a plan.
- If you want unlimited success, you need a limitless vision.
- Focus on what will work for you now.
- When you find an opportunity that aligns with your life plan, have confidence that your plan will succeed.
- If you are looking for direction, go to God in prayer.
- It takes courage, motivation, and focus to activate your plan.
- You can make a better-informed decision when you have all the data.
- You need wise and competent people giving you counsel.
- To step into your greatness:
    - Have a plan
    - Make decisions
    - Gather data
    - Be courageous enough to step out of your comfort zone
- When you consistently strive towards your purpose, you will begin to see supernatural doors open for you.

- Take your gifts to God in prayer. Ask Him to direct your steps.
- Your gifts were given to you to fulfill God's purpose.
- Life will sometimes be hard.
- Reignite your deferred dreams.
- You can, and you will overcome the hurdles that lay ahead.
- Greatness is possible.

References

Chapter 2: Decisions and Consequences

- Stossel, J. Sex in Middle School? https://abcnews.go.com/2020/story?id=123789&page=1. Retrieved July 20, 2018.

- Parental Support of Pregnant Teens. (n.d.) [Web log post]. Retrieved July 27, 2018 from http://www.teenpregnancystatistics.org/content/parental-support-of-pregnant-teens.html

Chapter 3: Fixed Windows

- BioMed Central. https://www.sciencedaily.com/releases/2010/07/100708193446.htm. Retrieved July 22, 2018.

- A Teen Pregnancy in the Family. (2015, July 21). [Web log post]. Retrieved from https://www.focusonthefamily.com/parenting/teens/your-teenager-is-pregnant/teen-pregnancy-in-family

Chapter 5: Passing the Test

- BioMed Central. https://www.sciencedaily.com/releases/2010/07/100708193446.htm. Retrieved July 22, 2018.

- Schuyler Center for Analysis and Advocacy. Teenage Births: Outcomes for Young Parents and their Children. (2008, December). Retrieved from http://www.scaany.org/documents/teen_pregnancy_dec08.pdf

- D.V. The Trinity of the Mind – The Conscious, Subconscious, and Superconscious Mind. (n.d.) [Web log post]. Retrieved May 3, 2018 from https://2empowerthyself.com/the-trinity-of-mind-the-conscious-subconscious-and-unconscious-mind/

Chapter 7: Confront and Release

- Amber, J. Engaging, Ensuring and Elevating: Essential Strategies for Mentoring Pregnant and Parenting Teens. (n.d.) Retrieved August 19, 2018 from https://nationalmentoringresourcecenter.org/images/PDF/Jeannine_AmberReport_Pregnant_and_Parenting_Teens.pdf

ABOUT THE AUTHOR

Kendra Hall is passionate about empowering teenage parents—especially young women—to reach their full potential. She offers invaluable insight and guidance that helps young women push through life's ebbs and flows and manifest their spiritual visions.

Ms. Hall is an active member of the Colorcomm Network, providing millennial mentorship as a ColorComm Fellow Coordinator. She also provides educational training to young women through the Pretty2Me Foundation.

Kendra has worked in state government for over 15 years and holds a bachelor's degree in Law and Justice.